MURDER & MAYHEM

—— IN ——

WASHINGTON COUNTY
RHODE ISLAND

KELLY SULLIVAN PEZZA

THE
History
PRESS

Published by The History Press
Charleston, SC 29403
www.historypress.net

Copyright © 2015 by Kelly Sullivan Pezza
All rights reserved

First published 2015

ISBN 978.1.5402.1277.1

Library of Congress Control Number: 2015939773

This book is dedicated to Frederick S. Kenney.
He was lucky enough to call this earth home for nearly one hundred years.
I was lucky enough to call him my friend.

CONTENTS

CONTENTS

ACKNOWLEDGEMENTS

I am forever grateful to the loyal readers of my weekly history column in the *Chariho Times*, especially Larry Webster and Hope Greene Andrews, who have been with me from the very beginning and have so lovingly offered their expertise on so many subjects; Jody Boucher and Matt Wunsch of Southern Rhode Island Newspapers for allowing me to do a job that I have loved every minute of; Pam Lavoie of Jules Antiques for her unending support and assistance; Joe Soares for all his help and kindness; KarenLu LaPolice for her generosity and contributions to this book; Janine Macomber for so graciously sharing her family history with me; Ricki Kenyon and Ken Hornik for always having the answers I need; the family of Fred Kenney for allowing me such precious time with their father; my daughter, Tatiana Maryhelen Pezza, for being such a wonderful little assistant; Tabitha Dulla and Katie Parry of The History Press for all your hard work; and all those individuals of Washington County who came and went before us, leaving us the heirs of their stories.

INTRODUCTION

S hortly after I was born, my mother began a postcard collection for me. Looking through it now, I see my adult interests mapped out by these cards so many years before I even had interests—the Lizzie Borden House, the Salem Witch Trials, the Newport Mansions and various other historical structures with fascinating tales attached to them. I wonder if it was mere coincidence that my mother chose such cards to collect for me or if she was actually predetermining what my future would hold.

Her own interest in history was spread to me at a very early age. I remember going to tour historical houses that were open to the public and tiptoeing around the outsides of old abandoned houses that were not. I remember toting paper and crayons to ancient cemeteries to do grave rubbings and reading the carved prose on the deteriorating stones.

I could not have been more than seven or eight years old when she first took me to South County Museum, and I found myself in a state of awe that I never knew existed—the old cars and kitchen implements, clothing and simple playthings; the matte visions of days past and the smell of history. Perhaps my passions were taught to me, or perhaps they were already in my blood, inherited from the blood of one who held the same passions.

I would later be shown notebooks that my mother had taken around to various Washington County cemeteries when she was a teenager, carefully listing the names and dates of those buried there; letters penned to her by a soldier who was eventually killed in Vietnam; and black-and-white photographs of relatives I never knew. History was simply a part of my day-

INTRODUCTION

to-day life, whether it was in the form of local legends, ghost stories or aged objects around our home that had sentimental tales attached to them. Going back into the past was as normal for me as moving toward the future.

So whether this love of history was carved into my DNA before I ever even took my first breath or the result of experiences, images and stories shared with me as a child, I am grateful to my mother for opening up such an incredible world to me—not only the world I live in but also the world as it once was. I can't imagine not being able to exist in both.

PART I
MAYHEM

DEVIOUS AND DISHONEST MAIDS
Locals Are the Victims of Their Own Housekeepers

We've all heard the saying "keep your friends close and your enemies closer," but back in the good old days, many people would have fared well to keep their friends close and their maids closer. Unfortunately, most did not. Benjamin Terry was a sixty-four-year-old retired cotton mill employee who resided in Wyoming, on the Hopkinton side of the river. After being widowed by Dorcas (Moon) in 1899, Benjamin's health began to fail, and he decided to hire a housekeeper. An honest, hard worker for many years, Benjamin had earned himself a beautiful, comfortable home and a worthwhile estate. A young woman known only as Miss Lacy soon arrived to take on the position of caring for Benjamin and keeping up his home.

In December 1900, a few concerned residents appeared at a town meeting and informed the council that Benjamin was very ill and his financial affairs were being mishandled. Evidence was given, showing that Benjamin was under the care of a physician and that he had been given a prescription for whiskey. Shortly after that prescription was filled, Miss Lacy had visited the doctor and told him Benjamin had used up the supply of whiskey and needed more. She then took the new prescription to a pharmacist, and noticing that no quantity was specified, she purchased a whole quart of the intoxicant.

According to those present at the town meeting, a little party was thrown at the sick man's house later that evening. Benjamin apparently was provided with very little of his "medicine." His concerned friends informed the council that he had gold in his house that they feared would be squandered. A former employer had paid Benjamin in gold pieces, which the ailing man had left in their envelopes and placed inside a small box. According to friends, he always left the top of the box open, unintentionally providing full access to the untrustworthy. The council was implored to appoint a suitable person to be named guardian over Benjamin's estate. Its request was granted, and Albert Lafayette Niles was given the position. There was a problem, however. Miss Lacy had already arranged for Benjamin to meet with a lawyer and draw up a will that left the entirety of his property to her. Miss Lacy felt she had a legal right to disperse money and goods in any way that suited her, as according to law, she was the new owner of the whole estate.

Such a trusting attitude also became the downfall of the Babcock family. Charles Babcock was a sixty-four-year-old farmer who resided in the Hopkinton section of Woodville with his wife, Annie. When the couple

The Woodville Mill stands amid the beautiful landscape of the village, where things weren't always what they appeared to be. *Vintage photograph courtesy of Joseph P. Soares.*

decided to employ a young girl to help out with household duties, they didn't have to look far. A twelve-year-old girl named Fannie lived nearby and agreed to take the job. Either the Babcocks didn't know of Fannie's reputation or didn't put much stock into it, but the girl was known to have a history of petty theft.

One day in October 1904, Charles came home and handed his wife two twenty-dollar bills to put away for safekeeping. Going into the sitting room, Annie placed the bills inside a glass ornament atop the fireplace mantel. Later in the day, when she went to retrieve them, one of the bills was gone. Annie remembered having sent Fannie into the sitting room to fetch something and wondered if her young employee had snatched the money. After telling Charles her suspicions, he began an investigation into the matter. It was discovered that, later that day, Fannie went to see Herbert Kenyon, the manager of a local mill, and showed him a twenty-dollar bill that she claimed to have found. She wanted to know if he thought it was real. Herbert looked it over and determined that it was, indeed, real. However, he remembered that his supervisor, Joseph Boland, had recently lost a twenty-dollar bill, so he went to him and reported his conversation with Fannie. Joseph tracked down Fannie, and she complied when he told her that the money was his, it had been lost and he'd like it back.

Charles reported his findings to fifty-six-year-old Constable George Harris Barber, who went to Fannie's home and asked to speak with her. Seemingly unbreakable, she swore that the money she had given to Herbert Kenyon was a bill she had simply found. As a result of the constable's pressured questioning, Fannie broke down and confessed that she had stolen the money from the Babcocks' sitting room. George proceeded on to Joseph Boland's house and explained to him that Fannie had admitted to theft and that the twenty-dollar bill could not have been the one he lost, as it belonged to the Babcocks. A short time later, Annie Babcock had possession of the money once again.

Household help stealing from their employers wasn't common, but it wasn't unheard of either. And with each local theft committed, families realized that they definitely needed to keep their maids close.

GREETING A TRAMP WITH KINDNESS LEADS TO TRAUMATIC EVENT FOR HARRIET BROWN

Elderly Woman Is Beaten by a Stranger

In this day and age, we are not quite as accommodating as our ancestors were. Should a stranger appear at our door asking for food, we would probably be on the phone dialing 9-1-1 before a full minute had passed. In earlier centuries, people were much more trusting. However, such willing acts of trust and kindness sometimes proved to be dire mistakes.

Everett Brown, a sixty-six-year-old picker-tender at a local woolen mill, wasn't home on Tuesday afternoon, February 18, 1919. His sixty-three-year-old Canadian-born wife, Harriet, was in the house alone that day when she suddenly heard a knock. She opened the door to find a tramp standing there and felt sympathetic when he asked her if he might have something to eat. Harriet invited the man out of the cold and into her warm home. He settled down at the kitchen table while she prepared a filling lunch for him. However, as hungry as he proclaimed to be, once he was served, he didn't eat much. He remained seated at the table for quite some time, despite his sudden apparent lack of appetite.

Having been most patient, Harriet finally asked him to kindly leave if he had satisfied himself. When the man failed to get up from the table, she asked him several more times to please vacate her residence. Finally, she gently took hold of him and attempted to move him toward the door. The twenty-five-year-old tramp immediately lunged into a brutal attack, physically injuring his gracious host quite severely. Instead of running off after the assault, he remained in the house for a good period of time. He stayed until nearly 4:00 p.m. before finally leaving the residence, which stood about a quarter mile away from Hopkinton City, and brazenly making his way toward Hope Valley.

Despite her injuries, Harriet immediately went for help, relaying what had just occurred to her sixty-year-old neighbor, carriage builder Roger Williams Lewis. Along with his son, Roger went to search for the man. They traced him to Hope Valley, where they alerted the constable to the crime that had been committed. Authorities apprehended the tramp just before dark in Richmond. He was arrested and placed in the Wyoming jail for the night. The following morning, he was transported to the jail at Westerly, where he gave his name as George Govan. He claimed that he was born in Iron Pond, Vermont, though authorities could find no

The dam at Wyoming, the bustling village where a tramp was incarcerated for attacking an elderly Hopkinton woman. *Vintage photograph courtesy of Hope Greene Andrews.*

such town in existence. He stated that he had been living with his sister in Lynn, Massachusetts. The tramp swore that he had never seen Harriet Brown before, but the woman positively identified him as the man who had assaulted her in her home.

Two months later, after a hearing in Superior Court, the accused was found guilty of the attack and sentenced to serve eight years in Rhode Island State Prison. At that point, authorities believed they could positively connect the man to another similar crime that had occurred in Massachusetts, and they made plans to bring up those charges at the time of his eventual release. Undoubtedly, the kindly intentions that came so naturally to Harriet Brown and others in the area were permanently scaled back after this traumatic event. Unfortunately, trust could not be given so freely, and sympathy could no longer come before personal safety—not even in a little country town where charity was a natural instinct.

ANIMAL CRUELTY

Residents Are Arrested for Animal Abuse

Despite the pleasant farms and warm-hearted rural folks, the behavior of Washington County residents in times past didn't always make for a pretty picture. On numerous occasions, the Society for the Prevention of Cruelty to Animals was called in to investigate the criminal, the heartless and the often grotesque actions of our townspeople.

In July 1900, police officer George Harris Barber, who also acted as an officer for the SPCA, was called to Woodville regarding a case of animal abuse. There, he discovered a horse lying beside the road in the hot sun, where it had remained for days. Carriage blacksmith Charles Sweet, a forty-three-year-old widower, had formerly owned the animal but sold it to Charles Burton. Sweet told Burton that the horse was aged but good enough for trips of about six miles or even getting to Westerly and back. Sweet wanted two dollars for the horse, and Burton agreed to pay that amount. However, as of that day, he had not.

Burton claimed that he discovered the horse was so old that it was absolutely useless and had returned the animal to Sweet two days later. Sweet refused to take the horse back and warned Burton that he had better make good on their deal. Burton stated that he would simply take the horse over to sixty-eight-year-old farmer Peter Palmer's place and leave it there. Sweet didn't care where he left the horse as long as he forked over the $2.00 he had agreed to pay. The two men couldn't come to an agreement, and Burton left. The horse stayed there by the side of the road, where it had been abandoned. The following day, the animal stumbled and fell. Too old and weak to get back on its legs, the horse dragged itself one hundred feet down the road. Officer Barber attempted to find someone who would be willing to care for the horse but was unsuccessful, so he had the animal shot. Sweet was prosecuted for animal cruelty and fined $17.70.

The following year, in April, Officer Barber arrested seventy-two-year-old farmer Ezra Holloway along with George W. Hopkins, both of Charlestown, after an agent for the SPCA made a complaint against the two men. They were charged with cruelty for failing to provide sufficient food and shelter for their horses. The next month, Charles Sweet took possession of Holloway's horse and was arrested by the SPCA once again. It was determined by the SPCA that the horse was unfit for labor. Sweet defended himself by claiming that he had not used the horse for labor due to the fact that he had no harness. By the time of the hearing, Sweet had already sold the horse to

In the olden days, most residents had animals of some sort, and the law tried to ensure that they were treated humanely. *Vintage photograph courtesy of Joseph P. Soares.*

a man in Plainville, who killed and buried it. Sweet found himself back in court, where he was fined and ordered to pay court costs, the total amount coming to $8.80.

Even domestic animals sometimes found themselves on the receiving end of cruelty. During the winter of 1902, it was discovered that some unknown person had shot the dog belonging to Dr. Edwards of Wyoming. The following day, the dog was still alive and suffering; it had crawled underneath the horse shed of the Hope Valley Baptist Church. An anti-cruelty officer was called in to investigate the matter, though the results of that investigation are unknown.

Albert C. Woodmansee of Richmond was arrested on the morning of June 10, 1908, by an agent for the SPCA after being investigated for failing to provide adequate sustenance for his horse for the previous five months. The fifty-two-year-old farmer pleaded not guilty and was hauled off to the Kingston jail to await a hearing.

John Rathbun Gorton of Hopkinton was unique in that he actually pleaded guilty to the charges that were brought against him in May 1905. Two complaints of cruelty had been made by an SPCA agent against the thirty-two-year-old lumberman. Gorton admitted that he did treat his horse quite harshly, as it was stubborn and he was determined to make the animal do what he wanted it to do. Despite his honesty, animal cruelty wasn't tolerated for any reason, and Gorton was fined $20.60.

When the Gypsies Came

Efforts Are Made to Keep Wanderers Out of Town

The word "gypsy" designates a person from a wandering ethnic race. Hailing from Asia, Ireland, India, Norway and a number of other countries, gypsies have existed for centuries, moving in caravans from one location to another in their nomadic lifestyle. "Gypsy" is derived from the word "Egyptian," where it is believed the travelers first originated. Romani, Domba and Banjara are just some of the many different gypsy ethnicities to be found throughout the world today.

Because of their mobile lifestyle, gypsies did not often hold down regular jobs. The men might find work doing day labor in the places they passed through, while the women were known for telling fortunes. Sometimes, the only way to provide for their large families was to steal. For that reason, gypsies earned a less than stellar reputation. In times past, the word "gypsy" was synonymous with all things unsavory. The pejorative word "gypped," meaning to be taken advantage of, derives from the belief that gypsies were unfair in their dealings.

There was a time when caravans of travelers passed through Hope Valley and surrounding villages. Like the residents of most other areas, no one welcomed their presence. Stories from the older residents in town inform us that whenever a caravan passed through, the adults would instruct the children to run, and everyone would begin shouting, "The gypsies are here!" It was not an event anyone welcomed but rather a reason for them to lock up their belongings and offspring.

On Monday, September 15, 1902, two caravans of gypsies passing through Hope Valley stopped to camp out for several days on the grounds of the Wood River Baptist Church. The following month, a caravan of Russian gypsies also passed through Hope Valley, headed in the direction of Westerly.

When summer arrived, the gypsies returned. On the Monday afternoon of June 22, a caravan stopped in Hope Valley, and several women emerged. They proceeded to walk around town, knocking on each and every door,

MAYHEM

asking if residents wanted their fortunes told. Before evening, they moved on to Ashaway, where they set up camp for a while.

On the afternoon of April 17, 1911, a Saturday, little Luther Dock of Hope Valley was riding his bicycle on High Street when he sped out in front of a gypsy wagon coming down the street. The horse knocked him down, and the wagon passed over him, causing bruises to his face and body. A male gypsy got out and attempted to care for the child until he could be carried home, where the doctor would soon treat him. As witnesses recalled the accident, it was evident the gypsy was not at fault, and he continued on is way.

Later that summer, on the Wednesday afternoon of July 12, six wagonloads of gypsies entered Hope Valley and came to a stop at Depot Square. It was said that a dozen women "in barbaric dress" came out of the wagons and went knocking on the doors of every house and business in town, offering to read fortunes. The male gypsies attempted to make deals in horse trading. Referred to as a "dirty and disreputable" bunch by the local newspaper, they came to the attention of Sherriff George Harris Barber, who ordered them out of town. Barber followed the wagons to the top of the hill, leading toward Ashaway, where he reminded them of their orders to vacate the town. Residents were warned by the newspaper that the gypsies "were apt to be suspected of light-fingered activity when the opportunity arises."

On Saturday evening, July 3, 1915, yet another gypsy caravan passing through Hope Valley decided to stop at Depot Square. Sherriff Barber immediately instructed them to move along. At first, the gypsies ignored him, but they finally retreated to their home on wheels and moved as far as the farm belonging to Roy Williard Rawlings in Richmond, where they again stopped. Rawlings contacted the police chief, who came and ordered them to leave. But the gypsies refused. They camped out there at the farm and left of their own accord the following morning. It was believed this group was just a small part of a very large caravan of nomads traveling together, though the others had set up camp for a week at Poquonock and had allegedly stolen from many henhouses and gardens in that area.

Reports of the travelers returning in July 1916 made the local newspaper. Three automobiles carrying a gypsy band drove through Hope Valley, and it was noted that their vehicles were brightly colored and in dilapidated conditions. The newspaper reported that the gypsies were "as disreputable in appearance as usual."

On Thursday morning, June 7, 1917, two more gypsy-filled automobiles stopped in Hope Valley and were soon hurried along by

19

An organ grinder, in full gypsy dress, performs at a street parade in Hopkinton in July 1921. *Vintage photograph courtesy of Hope Greene Andrews.*

Constable Matteson. A few weeks later, a group of them went into the grocery market of Mrs. Annie Carr, located on Nooseneck Hill in West Greenwich. Afterward, it was reported that while the clerk was in the rear of the store, one of the travelers stole a fountain pen valued at $3.50.

Despite the distrust and dislike of gypsies, it is interesting to note that occasionally their ways seemed to intrigue residents. On May 24, 1900, as visiting nomads strolled the streets of Hope Valley, proclaiming to know all things past and present, numerous residents approached them and handed over one dollar to have their fortunes told.

On the evening of Saturday, July 15, 1911, just three days after Sherriff Barber strongly ordered the band of nomads out of Hope Valley and watched them ascend the hill, a lawn party was held in Wood River Junction at the home of the wealthy Morse family—William; his wife, Caroline; their son, John; and their servant, Walter Clarke. Over five hundred guests attended, and one of the most popular events at the party was the fortunetelling being offered by gypsy Madam Von Siler. It was said that so many people requested to consult with her that by the time the party was over, some had not yet gotten their turns.

Eventually, gypsies were tolerated, if still not popular with the population as a whole. During World War I, a gypsy band stopped to camp at one of the travelers' favorite resting spots, the grounds of the Wood River Church. While it doesn't appear they were asked to leave, someone publicly raised the question of whether they had bothered to register for the draft.

At some point, the colorful caravans with their garishly dressed occupants stopped rolling through area towns. Nomadic women no longer strolled down the streets knocking on doors, and parents no longer told their children to run as neighbors screamed warnings about the arrival of the gypsies. However, a quiet intrigue of their lifestyle lingered. A few years after their disappearance here, a resident placed the following ad in the local newspaper: "Card reading by appointment, every afternoon except Sunday, by Madame A. Wright of Hope Valley."

THE PRESENCE OF THE KU KLUX KLAN
Local Involvement in the Infamous Prejudicial Group

The infamous white robes with pointed hoods are not specific to the South. Hundreds of people who regularly clad themselves in those robes used to walk down these local streets. Towering crosses that lit up the night sky were erected and set on fire right in our area fields. The men and women concealed beneath those hoods may have once lived in your house. They may have been your ancestors. They may have been locally prominent people, once praised by the community and now revered in our history for the philanthropy they eagerly demonstrated while unmasked.

Few people realize that the Ku Klux Klan was once a sizeable organization in this area, claiming hundreds of residents as members. Donning their white disguises, they followed the directions of their leader, as he preached hatred toward anyone who was not white, American and Protestant. The hierarchy of the KKK included captains, majors, generals and corporals. Each of these answered to the local KKK commander. The Reverend Edward Everett Knapp, a New York clergyman who was preaching in Connecticut, was serving as commander of Pequot Klan #13 during the 1920s. A divorcé, he had preached in Alaska, Wyoming and Colorado prior to relocating to the East Coast. Second in command to Knapp was "Major Bliven," with "Corporal Babcock" falling somewhat behind. According to the rules, the reverend was in control of issuing all orders concerning Klan #13.

One of the Klan booklets states:

The military committee of the individual Klan is the militant agency through which it will be possible for the Klan to operate and to execute the things desired by the members. Properly organized, it will be possible by this agency to reach every member of a Klan within a few hours. Careful attention should be given to the selection of subordinate officers, for a break in the chain would be fatal.

Attracting new members was very important. To determine a suitable candidate, individual town surveys were conducted to ascertain the number of Protestants, Catholics, foreigners and Klanspeople. The Ku Klux Klan was divided up into three sections—one for male members, one for the Women of the Ku Klux Klan and one for the Junior Prep, which trained children ages six to twelve. Junior members were ordered to wear armbands emblazoned with the letters J.P. White robes and headpieces called "helmets" needed to be purchased by each member and worn to rallies and meetings. One of the publications for members states that, in an effort to conceal the identity of the wearer without making the clothing unsafe, "the front apron shall have two holes of the proper size and location to facilitate the vision of the wearer."

Regular meetings of the Klan opened with everyone singing "The Star-Spangled Banner." As the meeting progressed, they would recite the "Pledge of Allegiance" and sing the patriotic tune "America." The Klan believed that devotion to the United States was of utmost importance and that the beliefs of Catholics, the entry of foreign citizens and the racial equality sought by African Americans would destroy the dignity of the country. The organization of these like-minded individuals sought to curb activities that would inevitably endanger or alter their patriotic visions. "The Klan is necessary to America if American principles, protestant ideals and white rule are to be preserved," one of its publications reads.

Some local people who were committed to the Klan eventually decided to opt out of membership. One Westerly woman who was very active in the Westerly Fire Department Ladies Auxiliary, Order of the Eastern Star, Easter Seals, American Legion Women's Auxiliary, the Red Cross, the Westerly Emblem Club, March of Dimes, the Woman's Relief Corps and the Central Baptist Church had served as secretary (otherwise known as the "kligrapp") of a local Klan. She penned the following letter to her fellow Klanswomen on October 21, 1929: "Please accept my resignation from the

A Connecticut man in Ku Klux Klan regalia believed in white supremacy, as did many in Washington County, Rhode Island. *Vintage photograph from the collection of the author.*

office of Kligrapp on Dec. 31st. At which time the books will be audited and ready to be turned over to the newly elected Kligrapp. This will give you ample time to secure a new secretary."

In 1926, a successful Westerly farmer penned a letter to Reverend Knapp, removing himself from the organization:

> *Am writing to inform you that from this day I do not consider myself a Klansman and also to hand in resignation as Captain of same. When I took my oath as a Klansman, I vowed to support superior officers and, if there was any differences, that I would leave the Klan and return all paraphernalia of the Klan. That is just what I am going to do. No more muddy or dusty roads for me. After listening to Rhodes talk in New London Saturday night, May 22, I feel convinced that he is not the type of man I wish to follow. It did my heart good to hear you, also Major Bliven. You had him covered at every turn. Any honorable man would have quit then and there but he not only refused to get out, but came at you with a cowardly blow that you had called the meeting together without singing America. How about the meeting at Bridgeport, when he forgot the benediction and the meeting was not officially closed? I joined the Klan because I thought it was right, and was ridiculed by my friends. I now think it is wrong and am willing to face more ridicule to do what I think is right.*

Discovered in a lonely farmhouse that time had seemingly passed over, these letters and publications are remnants of history that many of us are not eager to acknowledge. Among the yellowed paraphernalia is a small pamphlet that states, "For Commander Only! Caution! This secret work must be seen by no one except yourself! You will turn over to your successor in office this booklet and she shall work out the portions written in code. This booklet must be kept carefully concealed." Inside the pamphlet are secret codes and ciphers. It was to be "immediately burned" after being read. Those directions were obviously not followed, leaving us with an uncomfortably close look at the popularity of the Ku Klux Klan here in the North.

MAYHEM

The Attempted Abduction of
Teacher Mary Dahood
Woman Tries to Kidnap Teacher from Tomaquag

What began as just another day at school for students of Tomaquag Valley ended with an assault on their teacher, a police chase and an arrest. On the morning of October 8, 1917, lessons were proceeding as usual for the children who resided in Tomaquag. Suddenly, an automobile carrying several people pulled up in front of the door. The teacher, eighteen-year-old Mary Dahood, noticing the automobile and recognizing one of its occupants, quickly instructed two of the students to hurry to the nearby home of William L. Kenyon and come back with help.

She tried to keep her mind on her work, but the occupant she had recognized soon emerged from the vehicle and came into the schoolhouse. It was thirty-eight-year-old Hadla Dahood, who had emigrated with her husband and children from Beirut, Syria, in 1904. Hadla was Mary's mother and resided in Brooklyn, New York, where she operated a boardinghouse. A widow, Hadla had two other children—a nineteen-year-old and a thirteen-year-old. Hadla had placed Mary, her middle child, in a Norwich orphanage called the Rock Nook Home for Children several years earlier. Officials there would later say that she never kept in contact with the child until recently, when she had attempted to persuade her to come to Brooklyn and help out with the work at the boardinghouse.

Job Thorp, a native of England and prominent Westerly businessman, had become the legal guardian of Mary when she was a young teen and brought her from Rock Nook to live with him and his wife, Florence (Tucker). Hadla had tried to annul this guardianship but failed in her attempt so was now resorting to desperate measures. She walked to the front of the schoolhouse, grabbed hold of her daughter and pulled her from her chair. Hadla tried to drag Mary across the floor toward the door, but the girl sat herself firmly on the floor to gain resistance.

Soon, the two students Mary had sent for help returned with a number of men who thwarted Hadla's kidnapping efforts. Hadla returned to the waiting automobile and was whisked away. However, the sheriff soon caught up to them and placed Hadla under arrest for assault and creating a disturbance at a school. Hadla argued that her only intention had been to have a friendly talk with her daughter and that she had been sent on behalf of Mrs. John C. Averill, an official of the Rock Nook Home, who

Schoolchildren at Hope Valley Elementary School give the impression that every day in a rural school was typical. *Vintage photograph from the collection of the author.*

needed the girl to return to Norwich in order to sign some paperwork. When police contacted Averill, she said she had not sent Hadla on any errand to collect her daughter.

By 1920, Job and Florence had legally adopted Mary and changed her name to Mary Tucker Thorp. A successful and highly respected couple, Job sold plumbing supplies and household equipment. Florence had received a degree from Minnesota State University in 1904 and had been employed as a language teacher at the Williams Memorial Institute until her marriage. Their son Elliott would go on to become General MacArthur's chief of counterintelligence during World War II. When Job died in the summer of 1928, Florence went to live with Mary, who had already acquired her own share of success and esteem. In 1926, she had taken a teaching job at Rhode Island College and would remain there, filling positions, until 1962. She was later named the college's first distinguished professor and received the Roger Williams Medal and a commendation from Brown University for her community involvement.

A highly sought-after lecturer in the fields of education, health and child welfare, she was called to give the commencement speech to graduates of the Newport Hospital School of Nursing and to address varied women's groups on the subject of accepting one's true self. She went on to become principal of the Henry Bernard School at Rhode Island College, vice-president of the

Rhode Island Tuberculosis Association, president of the Rhode Island Lung Association, chairman of the Rhode Island Respiratory Disease steering committee and representative of the White House Conference on Children and Youth. She also served on the board of trustees at Saint Andrews School in Barrington and on the committee that set nursery school standards for the state of Rhode Island. In her honor, Rhode Island College developed the Mary Tucker Thorp Professorship Award, still presented annually to a deserving professor with at least six years of service at the college. In November 1961, the school dedicated a new dormitory called Mary T. Thorp Hall.

Mary became a naturalized citizen in September 1937 and a well-known author of numerous books regarding education. Her birth mother passed away on December 31, 1928, at home in New York, just five months after her adoptive father's passing. Florence died in July 1951. Mary Dahood, the little Syrian orphan, ended her life as Dr. Mary Thorp, an amazing woman who left a lasting impression on everything she touched.

CON ARTIST MANDEVILLE HALL TRICKS MULTIPLE WOMEN
Wealthy Man Deceives Every Chance He Gets

Co-owner of the Bentley-Clark Auto Company in Westerly, Benjamin Courtland Bentley, had been scammed, and he was not going to take it lightly. With what information he had on the swindler, Bentley drove from Watch Hill to Narragansett and got the police involved. Soon, the public would be aware that an international con artist had been having himself quite the party here in Rhode Island.

The scam artist was Mandeville de Marigny Hall, who was born on November 4, 1882. The son of William Cornelius Hall and Suzette de Marigny Thomas, he claimed to be a descendant of royalty. Whether or not that was true, Hall lived a privileged life. A graduate of Yale, he enjoyed the wealth and freedom that was afforded him. For Hall, money was no object—regardless of whose money it was. By the time he was a young man, he had written himself the history of a con artist.

In December 1905, Miss Lily F. Wilson of Kentucky announced that she had accepted a marriage proposal from Hall. She was aghast when,

Westerly was a busy, populated town, with many opportunities for a con artist. *Vintage postcard courtesy of KarenLu LaPolice.*

six months later, a notice appeared in the local newspaper stating that the engagement had been cancelled. Hall seemed shocked as well, accusing some unknown person of a "dastardly trick." However, the following month, while Wilson was vacationing in Paris with her mother, Hall exchanged vows with another woman, Miss Florence Teall of New York. Following the nuptials, he admitted that he was the person who had provided the newspaper with the notice concerning his engagement to Wilson.

One evening in January 1908, Hall was admitted to a New York hospital with a gaping wound in the right side of his body. He claimed that he had been cleaning his revolver at the home of his father when the gun accidentally discharged. Few believed him. It was well known that he had developed a drinking habit and that his marriage was on a downhill slide. Many believed that he had terribly botched a suicide attempt. Not long after his release from the hospital, Teall left him, telling family that she could no longer tolerate his drinking. Hall's solution to the dilemma was to simply get married again.

After becoming enthralled with a music hall chorus girl named Vida Whitmore, the two exchanged vows in New Jersey before heading off on a whirlwind trip to Paris. There, he purchased a $5,000 automobile from the Journey & Journey Company. He paid with a check, which was soon determined to be worthless. During a short jaunt to London, he was arrested and held for extradition. Once back in Paris, he was sentenced to thirteen months in prison for swindling. Whitmore was stranded there in France, having to contact friends and ask them to send her enough money to return home to New York aboard the *Lusitania*. Hall had taken away her jewelry during the trip and pawned it, explaining that he could not bear seeing her wear gifts that had come from other men. He kept the $8,000 profit, leaving her with nothing.

When Whitmore returned to New York, she learned that her husband already had a wife. Hall had never bothered to divorce Teall, who had hired an attorney since learning he was traveling with a woman who was claiming she was married to him. The marriage between Hall and Whitmore was annulled. That between Hall and Teall was ended through divorce proceedings. The twenty-seven-year-old con artist then went in search of Whitmore in hopes that she would remarry him legally. Whitmore had gone to Mexico and was letting a friend, Virginia Marshall, use her apartment. Marshall was a member of the Follies of 1909 and knew that Whitmore had no desire to be contacted by Hall. She was suspicious when a strange man calling himself Douglas Turner Johnston persisted in sending her notes and flowers, begging her to tell him where Whitmore was.

From New Haven, Hall sent Marshall a telegram asking her to call him at the New Haven House if she had no plans for the evening. Although she would later claim that she ignored the request, she received another telegram from Hall the following night, informing her that he would be leaving New Haven at 5:00 p.m. so that they could have supper in New York as agreed upon. Marshall met Hall for supper, and he brought her back to her apartment after midnight. The following day, he visited her again, once more asking questions about Whitmore's whereabouts. When Marshall didn't answer his questions, he asked her if she liked orchids. He then commenced to write out a check, which he handed to her. "Here's $250 for you," he said. He then took the check back, commenting that the amount was not enough. He tore it up and wrote out another check. "We'll make it $400," he said. He then asked her to accompany him back to New Haven. If she had been considering it, her suspicions were aroused again when she overheard a phone call he made to the Automobile Club. He explained to the person on the phone that he was sending his car there to have the gas tank filled. As his name was not on the club record, he stated that he was a new member and not on the books yet.

When Marshall went to cash the $400.00 check, the bank informed her that it was no good. Hall had convinced Marshall that he truly was Douglas

Turner Johnston, yet there was no checking account in that name. The owners of the Plaza Hotel soon realized they were victims of a con job, too, when the $23.00 check he had written them, signing his name as Douglas Johnston, was refused by the bank. Hall traveled on to Watch Hill. With his likable personality, good looks and expensive clothing, he confidently approached Benjamin Bentley, who owned a garage in the seaside community. Bentley didn't hesitate to grant Hall's request for an auto rental. Over the course of the next ten days, his bill had reached $175.00. By that time, however, the clock had once again begun counting down for the Ivy Leaguer. Realizing that it was not a good idea to keep signing his checks with the name of a nonexistent person, he decided to sign them with the name of a real man who had an account at the bank. Mr. A.E. Dick, the owner of the Watch Hill House, was given two checks by Hall, totaling $68.70, signed "Charles W. Stevens." Thanks to the keen eye of a bank clerk, it was noticed that the signature did not match that of Dr. Stevens. James M. Fuller, of Fuller's Detective Bureau, was sent for.

Fuller arrived in Watch Hill to find that Hall had left town two days earlier. Bentley had taken matters into his own hands and was already on Hall's trail. After learning that Hall had gone on to Narragansett, Bentley traveled to the pier. Word was that Hall had attracted the attentions of a hotel owner's daughter and was scheduled to meet her for dinner at eight o'clock that evening. Bentley contacted the chief of police, who stated that he would visit the meeting place at the appropriate time to arrest Hall. But it was James Fuller who got there first. He confronted the swindler and asked him if he was Mandeville Hall. Hall stated that he was not. Fuller informed him that he knew exactly who he was and who his father was. At that, Hall confessed to his identity. He was taken to the Kingston jail and placed on $1,000 bail for obtaining money under false pretenses.

A two-year stint in a Rhode Island prison did little to deter Hall from a life of crime. In 1915, he found himself behind bars once again after being sued by Florence G. Finch, whose father owned Finch Manufacturing Company in Scranton, Pennsylvania. She charged that Hall had sold stocks owned by her for $10,619 and failed to turn over any more than $500. A verdict was issued against him in October of that year. Seven months later, in desperation, Hall attempted to file for bankruptcy but was told that was something that couldn't be done after the fact. Mandeville Hall had finally come face to face with the reality that the adage "money is no object" certainly proved false, at least for him.

Dr. William Macomber Gets in Hot Water over Electrocure

Doctor Claims Machine Cures Disease

Dr. William Samuel Macomber left Hope Valley in 1896, moving out of the tenement he rented from Dr. Elisha Clarke to relocate to Illinois. The twenty-seven-year-old business-minded man was known for sporting a thick moustache, blond hair parted straight down the middle and tiny spectacles balanced on his nose. Always neatly dressed in a suit, he was the very picture of a successful doctor. A graduate of Hahnemann Medical College in Philadelphia, he had completed a full course of instruction in practical and surgical anatomy and a special course in practical obstetrics. The year before, he had received his license to practice medicine in Rhode Island. However, he strangely did not follow his chosen profession consistently.

In April 1893, he married a Massachusetts girl named Nellie Irene Lloyd. One week before their marriage, he penned her a letter from Hope Valley. "My dearest one, it is now nearly ten o'clock p.m.," he wrote. "One week from tonight at this time, if the Lord is willing, you and I will be man and wife and will be snug in your little home. It seems too good to be true. You asked if you might use the one dollar for some things you needed. Just as if it

William Macomber undoubtedly hoped his life would be quietly successful in peaceful Hope Valley, where even the village's Main Street gave one a sense of serenity. *Vintage photograph courtesy of Hope Greene Andrews.*

Dr. William Macomber and his wife in 1913. *Vintage photograph courtesy of Janine Macomber.*

wasn't just as much yours as mine. Of course you can. Use it just as you please." Explaining that he had planned on letting her handle the family pocketbook, Macomber was clearly a loving husband and successful provider. He and Nellie went on to have two children—Grace in 1895 and Harold in 1898—and after residing for some time in Illinois, he decided to take on another line of work. He began working as a traveling tool salesman and apparently enjoyed that work, as he continued doing it when he and his family returned to Rhode Island a few years later, settling down in Providence.

Around 1906, however, the Rhode Island Board of Health discovered that he was selling a certain "tool" that was of great concern to it. More like a machine than a tool, the "Electrocure" was an apparatus that, its makers claimed, would cure everything from constipation to cancer. It was advertised that when the device was placed in water, the water was charged with oxygen and produced medicinal qualities in which the patient would then bathe. Other doctors around the country had been helping to sell the Electrocure as well.

When the Rhode Island Board of Health discovered that Macomber was passing out flyers that advertised the Electrocure over the name "W.S.

Macomber, M.D.," it took immediate action. A chemist was instructed to test the device and came to the conclusion that no electricity was generated when it was put into water. He also found that the "medicinal" water patients were bathing in was no different from any other water. After a ruling that Macomber was guilty of "gross unprofessional conduct and of conduct of a character likely to deceive and defraud the public," his license to practice medicine in the state of Rhode Island was revoked.

Macomber was not happy about this ruling and wasn't going to accept the loss of his license without a fight, especially since he felt he offered compelling evidence in his favor. He had supplied the board with fifty witnesses, patients who had agreed to come and speak about how they had been cured or relieved of their inflictions by Electrocure. When the board agreed to hear testimony from just ten of those people, Macomber decided to file an appeal with the Supreme Court in Providence. In the summer of 1906, the Supreme Court overruled the decision by the Board of Health, reinstating Macomber's medical license. The judge stated that there was no evidence to show that statements made by him were untrue or even misleading. He and his family continued living in Providence until just before 1920, when they moved to Ohio. The dashing doctor apparently remained there, selling tools—instead of practicing medicine—for the rest of his life and died in the spring of 1936.

Two Local Doctors and Their Dalliance with Drugs
Medicine Men Risk Their Jobs over Drug and Alcohol Abuse

Locals depended on the care and advice of area doctors to keep them in the best of health. However, it might have been quite uncomfortable to call on a physician who was known for having a drug or alcohol problem. On the Tuesday evening of July 17, 1900, Mary Farrell of Westerly contacted the police. Her husband, Dr. Henry W. Farrell, had seemingly disappeared from their home, and she was very worried. The doctor maintained an office at the Banigan Building at the bottom of College Street in Providence. The ten-story, steel-frame building covered in granite was considered to be the city's first skyscraper.

Authorities in Westerly contacted Officer George Harris Barber of Hope Valley, who immediately began to search for Farrell. After just a short time, he was able to locate the doctor at Mulholland's Saloon in Wyoming, a structure that still stands along Main Street. John Mulholland and his wife, Minnie, were boarders at the home of Minnie's seventy-two-year-old grandfather Edmund Jordan. Jordan had numerous run-ins with the law concerning his sale of illegal alcohol, and now his grandson-in-law was running a saloon of his own.

Barber got back to Westerly authorities and assured them that the doctor was undoubtedly going to be staying at the saloon all night and they could all deal with it in the morning. The officer went to bed but was later roused when he was contacted once more and informed that Mrs. Farrell was not at all satisfied. She was greatly concerned about the horse and buggy her husband had taken with him, as they belonged to her sixteen-year-old daughter, Annie. She wanted the police to go and take possession of them. Barber assured her that the horse and buggy would not be moved until the morning, and Mrs. Farrell could come and take possession of them herself at that time.

The Wood River Branch depot in Hope Valley, where the wife of Dr. Henry Farrell disembarked to collect her intoxicated husband. *Vintage photograph courtesy of Hope Greene Andrews.*

The first train to Hope Valley the following morning carried the doctor's wife and daughter. Farrell remained at the saloon, where he had become absolutely penniless. The horse and buggy had been boarded, and two days' worth of charges were now due. Mrs. Farrell paid the charges, and the horse and buggy were taken to Barber's stable until she could arrange for their transport to Westerly. When the 10:25 a.m. train left Hope Valley, Mrs. Farrell and her daughter were on board, toting home the hungover physician.

On the morning of October 19, 1925, Dr. Herbert Enoch Rouse of Shannock stood inside the Second District Court and pleaded *nolo contendre* to a charge of operating a vehicle while under the influence of narcotic drugs. The fifty-five-year-old physician had attended the University of Vermont and received his medical degree from the Baltimore College of Physicians and Surgeons in 1896. He had first worked as a surgeon for the BR&P Railway and then as a doctor for the U.S. Navy. In 1898, he had come to Shannock and started a private practice there. He went on to become medical examiner for the towns of Richmond and Charlestown. On September 29, 1902, Rouse married Hortense James, who died two years later. He then married Marion Lewis in 1906, but the union ended in divorce. In the publication *History of the State of Rhode Island and Providence Plantations*, a glowing biography is given of Dr. Rouse, stating that he "earned a splendid reputation" for the high standards of his profession. Rouse was given a fine of fifty dollars plus court costs for driving while drugged and severely reprimanded by the judge, who assured him that he would be given a jail sentence if it happened again.

TALENTED SWINDLER OR DESPERATE TRAVELER?
Stranger Makes Off with the Money of Locals

One cold day in February 1876, a neatly dressed man was traveling on foot from Voluntown, Connecticut, toward the village of Rockville. Along the way, he stopped at a farmhouse and asked the owner how close to Rockville he actually was. In the course of the conversation, the man learned that there was a Seventh-Day Baptist church in the village. He was given the names of some of the parishioners and continued on his way, making a point to seek out one of them. After arriving in Rockville, he did just that. He introduced himself to the parishioner as H.G. Warren and said he resided in Plymouth, Massachusetts. "My father has been a Seventh-Day Baptist for

Even in rural villages like Rockville, being too trusting could prove to be a downfall. *Vintage photograph from the collection of the author.*

fifteen years," he related. "My mother has always been one. I have been one for five years."

Warren went on to convey how happy he was to meet the Rockville resident. "It seems like being among my own folks," he said. The stranger claimed that he worked as a miller but had been sick and was staying in Stafford Springs, Connecticut, to regain his health. Now he was anxious to return home but was facing a problem. "I spent most of my money," he told his new acquaintance. "I sent to my father for a remittance, but the letter must have miscarried as I did not hear from him." Warren said that when he left Stafford Springs, after paying for his room at the boardinghouse, he had but one dollar and ten cents in his pocket. "Learning of your church in this place, I have called upon you, hoping you would make me a small loan to help me to reach my home." Warren held up one misshapen hand. "This is the sign of a miller," he explained. "All millers have a crooked hand, caused by striking the measure in taking toll."

The Rockville resident could not subdue his sympathy. He reached into his pocket and pulled out two dollars, which he handed to the stranger. Warren eagerly expressed his gratitude. "I will send the money back by return mail, and you will have the money in your pocket again by the last of the week," he said. "I will put a stamp on the letter so that you can write to me that you received the money all right." He added that his father would most likely put in his own words of thanks as well. "And this will be the means of opening up a communication between families of kindred faith," he said. The Rockville resident, so glad for being able to alleviate the worries of this poor traveler, now wanted to do even more for him. As it was almost lunchtime, he invited the man to dine with him at his house. "Thank you," Warren said. "But I am in a hurry to get on my way home." With that, he began walking toward Hope Valley.

It wasn't long before he centered his attention on the mill in the distance. He stopped and engaged in conversation with the mill owner. "My father owns a mill that runs three sets of stones," he announced. "Also a shoddy mill and is taxed at $30,000." He explained that he was sick and on his way home but had run out of money. "I failed to get a remittance from my father and have ventured to call on you, as a brother miller, knowing that millers sympathize with each other in trouble." The mill owner replied that he was aware Warren was asking him for money but that he had been scammed once before. "I loaned a man a dollar to help him get home as he said and never heard from him or the money afterward."

Warren expressed great disgust in reaction to the story. "That was downright rascality of the worst type," he said. "It is calculated to close the doors of charity against worthy objects. Such imposters should be treated with the utmost rigor of the law." The mill owner began to feel that it was wrong to deny help to a needy man due to the actions of another. He reached into his pocket, pulled out four dollars and handed the money to Warren. The traveler could not thank him enough and finally offered to leave his expensive coat as collateral. The mill owner refused. After hearing about how sick Warren had been, he was not about to take his coat on such a cold day. "This money I will return by Friday night," Warren promised. "And my father will put into the letter one or two dollars extra for the kindness you have shown his son." He then continued on his way.

The weeks came and went, and there was no correspondence from Warren sent to Rockville or Hope Valley—no letters and no money. Many area residents decided that the two generous men had been swindled by a con artist. But there were others who chose to believe that the stranger had mailed the money as promised and that the letters had been lost somewhere along the way. Still others thought perhaps Warren's illness had worsened as he made his way home and he had died prior to reaching his destination.

Respectable Champlin Family Tale Begins to Twist
Local Man Attempts to Poison Family

John Segar Champlin of Hopkinton worked hard to establish his reputation. A successful businessman who incorporated work, religion and family into his life, he was the husband of Abby Spicer, who hailed from an esteemed family in her own right. Among their children was Thomas Francis Champlin, born on March 2, 1848. A lifelong farmer, Thomas married Alma F. Crumb in 1870 and went on to raise a family of nine children. It was during this time that the respectable tale of the Champlin clan began to twist and turn.

Thomas and Alma had a son, Thomas Elijah Champlin, who was born on February 19, 1875. They also had a daughter, Mabel Amelia Champlin, born on October 1, 1880. Mabel had won the heart of a local man named William Jacques, and neither the younger Thomas nor his father was happy about this. In the summer of 1897, the elder Thomas had verbally and physically threatened William to stay away from his daughter and never set foot in their home in Hopkinton City again. William ignored the warnings and continued coming to the house to court Mabel as usual. On July 6, 1898, the two young lovers decided to elope. William picked up Mabel at her father's home in his carriage, and the pair traveled to Milltown, Connecticut, where they were married. At midnight, they returned to the residence, having decided that Mabel would spend a few more days at home before moving in with her new husband. But the teenage girl's father was waiting, and his twenty-three-year-old son, Thomas, stood at his side. As the elder Thomas yelled at William, he forcefully took physical possession of his daughter, as well as the horse and carriage. Meanwhile, the younger Thomas threw William to the ground and proceeded to kick him in the face, head and body. A very religious man who did not believe in violence, William made no attempt to fight back. Once the attack subsided, he pulled himself up and began to walk home. His face was gruesomely disfigured, covered with blood and bruises.

As William neared the village of Hope Valley, he crossed paths with the younger Thomas, who was driving his horse and carriage. Thomas apologized for the attack and stated that he only wanted to return the possessions. William accepted the offering and rode home to Spring Street. The following morning, the elder Thomas threw Mabel out of

Spring Street in Hope Valley, where the love-struck William Jacques lived. *Vintage postcard courtesy of Hope Greene Andrews.*

the family home, and she moved in with William. The couple went on to have two children.

The younger Thomas, however, had shown evidence of his dark side. Four years later, in the summer of 1902, he arrived unannounced at the home of Charles Scott in Pawcatuck. Mr. Scott was not home that Monday evening, and his wife was entertaining a guest, Eunice Corey. The only recognition Mrs. Scott had of Thomas was that he used to visit her grandfather. She had no idea why he was suddenly at her house, appearing to be very drunk. When he began using foul language in his conversation, Mrs. Scott threatened that she would call for someone to come remove him from the property. Thomas warned that if she called for anyone, he would throw them over the back stair railing, which was fifteen feet from the ground. Mrs. Scott tried to reason with him, explaining that if he did any such thing, he would end up in jail. "I would go to jail as well as anywhere else," he smugly replied. He then pulled a small bottle out of his pocket. "This is poison," he told the women. They could clearly see it contained white powder and was affixed with a poison label. "My employer, John Champlin, ordered me to get it to kill crows," he said. "What could be held on the point of a knife would be enough to put you out of business." His threat made clear, he slipped the bottle back into his pocket.

At about ten o'clock that evening, Mr. Scott returned home, and Eunice left. Mr. Scott had never met Thomas before and conducted himself in a charitable manner when the young man asked if he could spend the night. Mrs. Scott awoke at about four o'clock the next morning, hearing sounds coming from the kitchen. She roused her husband, and he found Thomas rifling around in the pantry. Thomas explained that he was making himself something to eat and then going on to work. However, he immediately left without any breakfast. Later that morning, Mrs. Scott went into the pantry to find white powder scattered all over the counter, around the sink, on the sugar jar and over a plateful of steak. There were also powdery fingerprints on the cupboard door. She thought it was perhaps flour but noticed a difference in the color when she compared the two.

That evening, Eunice returned once again to have dinner with Mrs. Scott. Two hours later, she fell violently ill. Dr. Payne was called, and observing what he assumed to be symptoms of poisoning, he removed some food from the house for chemical analysis. It was found to contain arsenic, and Thomas was promptly arrested.

In August 1914, Thomas was arrested again, this time for assault with a dangerous weapon. Previously that day, he had engaged in an argument with James Gagnon, whom he accused of stealing his dinner pail while he was hauling wood to Bradford. The argument turned into a physical fight, with James coming out the victor. Later, with a shotgun in hand, Thomas marched onto the property of James Girard, where George and James Gagnon were camped out with Philip Alberts. He riddled a nearby building with bullets while threatening to kill all three of them. When he ran out of ammunition, the trio ran for their lives while Thomas quickly reloaded his weapon. Joseph Bushee, who lived nearby and heard the commotion, rushed over and attempted to talk some sense into the gunman. Thomas aimed the gun at Bushee and began to fire as Bushee ran away under a hail of bullets, some of which pierced his hat. Police later arrested Thomas at his home and transported him to Westerly for arraignment. Even the most respected clans have their skeletons lurking somewhere in the family tree.

MAYHEM

PUTTING AN END TO COCKFIGHTING
Raid on Illegal Gambling Is Cause for Commotion

The carriages bumped along the rutted dirt road as the men they carried held their breaths in anxious anticipation. It had taken a lot to get them all assembled that night. They arrived in Richmond, via both horse and train, from all over Rhode Island. Some weren't even told exactly where they were going in order to keep the mission as quiet as possible.

James N. Smith, state agent for the Anti-Cruelty Society, led the many police officers who had come to assist him down the remote winding roadway. It was about 11:30 p.m. on Saturday, May 23, 1903. Smith had just gotten word that morning concerning the violent event that was to take place at Mort Cross's Shannock farm that very night. A stealth plan was quickly put into place in order to stop it.

As the men arrived at the Cross property, they could see a dwelling house with a barn behind it. In front of the house was a makeshift saloon, where much local trouble had already originated. A great deal of excited noise was coming from the area of the barn, and the assembly headed in that direction. As the barn door was opened to permit their entrance, the agents and officers observed a large group of men surrounding a twelve-foot-square pit. The pit was enclosed by boards about two feet in height, and four large Rochester lamps hung over it, causing a bright glare that lit the entire room. Inside the pit, two roosters were violently disfiguring each other. As blood spattered and feathers flew, the men who were gathered around cheered loudly.

Squirrelly henchmen had been stationed at all points of entry, and the guard at one door, not knowing it was the law who stood before him, asked the newly arrived men to pay the regular spectator fee of two dollars. The officers and agents ignored the request and proceeded to enter the barn. "Stop!" Smith yelled loudly. "You're all pinched!"

The clamor was suddenly reduced to silence. Some of the men sat still and scared, while others, upon realizing what was happening, decided to make a run for it. Within seconds of Smith's announcement, the silence was gone once again and the air wrought with noisy confusion. Smith fired his pistol into the air. "I don't want to shoot anybody, but if it's fighting you want, we're ready for you!" he warned. Silence quickly returned.

One large man, Delmonico Clarke of Charlestown, brazenly walked toward an exit. An officer swung his eighteen-inch-long nightstick, hitting Clarke so hard across the cheek that he spun like a top to the floor. He was soon handcuffed. Winfield Scott Chappell of Westerly, who had been one

The mill in Shannock, a wooded village that wasn't able to conceal its secrets well enough. *Vintage postcard courtesy of Hope Greene Andrews.*

of the principals in the cockfight, suddenly turned and climbed through an open window, jumping twenty feet to the ground below. A whack from a nightstick as he jumped made his projection shaky, and he landed in a pile of rough stones. One of the officers raced outside and fired his pistol into the air as Chappell ran into the woods. Another man, who was in the process of climbing up onto a windowsill, was struck across the back with a nightstick just as the pistol shot rang out. Thinking the blow to his back was a bullet, he fell onto the barn floor, screaming, "I'm shot! I'm shot!"

"They're blank shots," one bold spectator announced as police cuffed him and his comrades. "Don't be afraid."

Another wasn't so brave. "Don't think they're blanks, boys," he advised. "Don't give them a chance to hit you. You might as well give up."

One gambling man quietly slipped into the area of the chicken coop and began prying a board from the wall. After much work, he managed to move the board enough to get one leg through. An officer standing outside had silently watched the labor and now struck the man's leg with his nightstick, causing him to withdraw the throbbing limb. Yet another was found hiding deep within the haymow. As the police worked to contain the fifty or so men, Delmonico secretly worked at his cuffs with a pocketknife, severing one of them. Police noticed and fitted him with a new pair.

Among the evidence confiscated were two copies of an agreement, written out on paper bearing the letterhead of Alexander Morrissey. A resident of New London, thirty-three-year-old Morrissey was a well-known promoter of sporting events that included cockfights, animal racing and boxing bouts. In addition, he owned horses and was a dog breeder and trainer. A busy man, Morrissey also ran a saloon on Bank Street in New London.

"We, the undersigned, agree to fight on the night of the 23rd day of May, 1903," the agreement read. "A main of seven cocks for the sum of fifty dollars a side, plus gate receipts. Winner take all." The agreement went on to state that the pit would be made of dirt and well lit with at least two Rochester lamps. "Boston rules to govern battle," it went on, explaining what was allowed concerning the weight of the spurs. "The fight shall take place at Mort Cross's place in Shannock, RI. Referee shall be agreed upon at pit site. Fifteen dollars will be taken from gate receipts for Mr. Ring's expenses." It was dated May 4, 1903, and signed by Winfield Chappell, Alexander Morrissey and Edward Ring.

Edward A. Ring was a Willimantic resident who owned eight of the birds involved in the evening's fight. He refused to give his name during the raid but was arrested anyway. Chappell managed to escape. In all, forty-seven men were taken into custody, the majority of them hailing from New London. In the morning, twenty-five of the men were fined eleven dollars each for attending the brutal blood sport. Ring was fined a total of fifty-seven dollars for his involvement, which included owning and training fight birds.

It was discovered that Ring had made the acquaintance of another spectator from Westerly, James L. Sisson, in a saloon in New London on May 2. Conversation led them to arrange the cockfight. Such fighting was illegal. As roosters are aggressive toward one another by nature, those involved in the sport would breed and train birds to be especially violent. Fitted with sharp spurs on their feet, two roosters at a time would be put into a ring to tear each other apart until one was dead. When the agents arrived that evening, the fight was already in its second bout. Sixteen live birds were confiscated while the two in the process of fighting were so disfigured that they were shot by police to end their suffering.

Morrissey died in the spring of 1915 at the age of forty-five from heart-related problems, but illegal cockfighting continued to draw crowds into the shadowed recesses of Rhode Island. And Mort Cross's property, with its makeshift saloon, continued to be the location for activities patrons didn't want police to be aware of.

In Narragansett with a Plan to Kill Edward Everett Hale

Intending to Murder a Famous Writer, a Man Rents a Room in Narragansett

William Armistead Collier Jr. left his home in Memphis, Tennessee, to start a new job in advertising on the East Coast. An intelligent twenty-three-year-old man with a wonderful upbringing, he loved to read about theology and took a special interest in the book *A Man without a Country*, written by Unitarian clergyman Edward Everett Hale of Boston.

Hale had been a child prodigy who enrolled in Harvard at the age of thirteen and went on to graduate second in his class. In 1846, he was licensed to preach and supplied the pulpit around Massachusetts. He and his wife, Emily (Perkins), raised eight sons and one daughter while he found fame penning American masterpieces, founding magazines and publishing a wide assortment of articles and short stories.

It was the summer of 1897 when Collier decided to seek out the religious author and introduce himself. During their meeting, he told Hale that he hoped to become a missionary someday, and the reverend immediately felt a great eagerness to help him achieve that goal. Hale secured a room for the young man at Hale House, a college settlement, where he was provided with living quarters free of charge. Little did anyone know that they were assisting Collier in reaching a goal much different than that of a missionary.

Collier had been at Hale House for only a week when the superintendent discovered him stealing another's food from the refrigerator. When he was asked not to help himself anymore, he became so enraged that he stormed away from Hale House. A few days later, the superintendent received a letter from Collier that had been sent from Narragansett. In it, he threatened to kill the man for insulting him. The superintendent quickly contacted Hale and informed him of the contents of the letter. Hale was not surprised. He had been receiving strange letters from Collier as well. In those letters, Collier claimed to be the Messiah and stated that unless Hale converted to his cause, he would take his life.

To Hale, these were just the ravings of a lunatic. However, the lunatic was not in Boston where Hale had left him. He had followed the clergyman to the Hale family summer home in Matunuck, renting sleeping quarters from fifty-two-year-old Matilda Emma (Clarke) Knowles, who owned the cottages at Druid's Dream in Narragansett. He told Mrs. Knowles little about himself except that he was engaged in very important work. He

The plaque on Druid's Dream, the Narragansett estate built by Joseph Peace Hazard in 1884, where murderous William Collier plotted the death of author Edward Everett Hale. *Photograph taken by the author.*

stayed in his room writing most of the time, but when he did emerge, he complained about terrible pains in his head. In addition, he usually refused to eat any of the meals Mrs. Knowles brought to him. At one point, she suggested it was in his best interest to eat something. "You do not know whom you are talking to," he told her. "I am the second Messiah, and I have come to redeem the world."

One afternoon in August, Collier received a letter and became extremely agitated. Early the next morning, he left the premises of Druid's Dream,

The Edward Everett Hale house in Matunuck, summer residence of the theologian and author. *Vintage postcard from the collection of the author.*

telling Knowles he would return soon. After his departure, Knowles entered his room and looked down at the letter on the desk. It was from Hale. "You have two diseases," it read. "One is what the world calls conceit. The other is laziness. You had better go to work."

Hale's wife looked out her window later that day to see a strange man lurking around the property. She immediately called the police, and an officer arrived to find Collier hiding in the woods. A terrible fight ensued that caused scalp wounds to the officer before he was able to overtake Collier and secure him. When he arrived at the jail in Kingston, Collier talked incessantly. He admitted that he'd traveled to Rhode Island for the purpose of assassinating Hale. "He has been teaching a false religion," he explained. "He is an imposter, and I am going to shed his blood. I'm the second Messiah. I'm Christ, who has come into the world to shed the blood of sinners even as Jesus Christ shed his blood for us."

Witnesses said that calm statements would be followed by spells of wild ravings. Realizing that something was seriously wrong with his mental state, authorities contacted his family. His father, a United States colonel, as well as an attorney, was a highly respected man. He stated that he had been searching for his son and was aware that he was crazy. He asked that the young man be placed in an asylum until transportation back to Memphis could be arranged. Collier was thereby locked safely away and Hale spared his life.

Collier died of a heart attack in 1947 at the age of seventy-three. Hale went on to accomplish many more literary successes in the world of theology. In 1903, he was named chaplain of the United States Senate and died six years later in Boston.

POLICE OFFICER GEORGE BARBER SOLVES HEN MYSTERY

Woman Admits She Poisoned Her Neighbor's Chickens

Emma Baggs threw some feed to her flock of chickens early on the morning of July 25, 1900. The forty-seven-year-old had never married or had children, so she spent the majority of her time working around the house and small farm in Wood River Junction. The eldest child of John Baggs and Rebecca (Drown), she had lost her mother when she was just seventeen. Her maternal aunt Sally Church had lived with the family since becoming a young widow many decades earlier. Now, Emma cared for the eighty-one-year-old lady in the downstairs tenement they shared.

Nearly every family residing in rural villages, such as Rockville, kept chickens in their yards. *Vintage photograph from the collection of the author.*

At about eleven o'clock that afternoon, Emma passed by the chicken coop again and noticed that something was drastically wrong with the flock, which had been in a lively, healthy condition just hours before. Two of the chickens lay dead in the pen, while the others stumbled around as if they had been drugged, showing obvious signs of sickness. Emma noticed many lumps of strange-looking dough scattered inside the coop. She knew she hadn't thrown it inside, so she sent for Officer George Harris Barber of Hope Valley. Barber arrived at the property the next day and investigated the grounds. After entering the barn that stood beside the coop, he discovered two boxes of Paris green, a pesticide commonly used by farmers at that time. However, the boxes had not yet been opened.

Barber continued to walk around the premises, carefully looking through the bounty growing in the garden and the recesses of outbuildings for some clue about what might have been in the dough thrown to the chickens and whom the culprit might be. Finally, as he was making his way toward a small children's playhouse in the yard, he noticed a tin pail just outside it. In the pail was a small amount of dough made from northern meal bran. Paris green had been mixed into it.

Barber decided to question the family who lived in the apartment above Emma. Thirty-seven-year-old Asiel Burnside Kenyon, a railroad employee, resided there with his wife of thirteen years, Martha Ann (Larkin), aged thirty-five. Upon Barber's arrival, he found only Martha and the couple's three children—Iva, Anna and Jarvis, who ranged in age from five to eleven—at home. Two other children had previously passed away. Barber asked Martha if she knew anything about Emma's chickens being poisoned. She adamantly swore she had no knowledge of it. Barber spent a great deal of time trying to get Martha to confess; however, she maintained her innocence. When Barber decided to tell her that he had proof she was the culprit, she finally announced herself as being guilty of the act. She explained how she had mixed up the dough and the poison and fed it to the hens. When Barber asked her why she would do such a thing, she stated that she didn't know why she had done it.

The Kenyon family eventually moved to Massachusetts and had two more children. Asiel continued working for the railroad. Emma Baggs married woolen mill weaver Seth Higgins in 1909 at the age of fifty-six, becoming his second wife. Unfortunately, he passed away two years later. It's not known whether Emma ended up losing her entire flock in the Wood River Junction chicken-poisoning incident, but it's almost certain she kept her eyes on her upstairs neighbor in the days that followed.

JOHN CROSS TRIES HIS BEST
TO END GAMBLING AT NARRAGANSETT PIER

Illegal Gambling Becomes Pastime
of the Narragansett Elite

Narragansett attorney and constable John G. Cross thrust his arms into a long raincoat. He perched a slouchy hat atop his head, completing the look of a sleuth. He grabbed a blackjack and then an axe, finally setting out on his mission. Cross arrived in Wakefield at 11:00 p.m. to meet up with some other men: fifty-two-year-old attorney William Mills Ivins and his twenty-three-year-old son, James, both hailing from East Twenty-fifth Street in Manhattan and staying at their summer home in Earl's Court; George L. Cutting of Massachusetts; and two fellow local constables, Samuel Brown and George Tenant. It was almost time to put the evening's plan into action.

Cross was a highly determined twenty-seven-year-old who lived with his parents on Pier Road in Narragansett. Not content to merely fight for the rights of his clients on a case-by-case basis, he was vigilant in his desire to actively uphold the law in any and all circumstances. He and those who gathered with him on the Saturday evening of August 7, 1910, had long been on a public tirade concerning gambling. It was well known that Narragansett Pier was a mecca for the illegal activity, and the local police apparently did little to squash it. Cross and other Narragansett residents and summer visitors despised the stain that threatened to blot out their picturesque beachfront wonderland. So now they were going to take matters into their own hands.

The Narragansett Club, run by William Arnold, was highly suspected by Cross and his men for housing a veiled gambling operation. At seven minutes past midnight on August 8, 1910, the group approached the front door of the club, where a doorman met them. William Ivins restrained the man while Tenant went inside, followed by the others. They ascended a staircase that led to a long, narrow corridor. Arriving at a foyer, they pushed open the door and entered a room that rang with laughter and carefree gaiety. The men entered and gazed around, their presence completely unacknowledged. The large room was elaborately decorated with expensive furnishings and wall hangings. Proper women draped in the latest fashions primly worked their way around the room, while well-suited millionaires indulged themselves in the camaraderie of the rich. The room was neatly laid out with roulette wheels, in almost constant motion as the jet set tried their luck. One large table was set up for a card game, while

Narragansett Pier was a magnet for the wealthy, who often thought rules didn't apply to them. *Vintage postcard from the collection of the author.*

another gaming table incorporated dice. The gleaming floor was strewn with colorful gambling chips and discarded scorecards.

Cross and his crew loudly introduced themselves and demanded that everyone stop what they were doing and assemble in a corner of the room. Cross then attempted to obtain the names of all in attendance, allowing each to leave the premises after complying. Many of the forty or so present provided false names before departing from the club. For the next hour, the raiders held down the fort in order to keep their eyes on the gambling paraphernalia, which was hard evidence of the illegal activity taking place there. With a revolver in his hand, Cross crossed the room, retrieving chips and cards from the floor and shoving them into his pockets. Now and then, a waiter or two would enter the room to collect glasses or clean tables. Suddenly, Cross noticed that, little by little, the evidence was disappearing and realized the employees were whisking it away behind his back.

Constable John Cullen soon arrived and attempted to place Ivins under arrest. Cutting quickly jumped between the two men, hitting Cullen over the head with a revolver to prevent him from hauling Ivins away. The police chief was next on the scene, as was the club owner. Cross admitted he had not obtained a warrant before conducting the raid. Cutting was arrested on a charge of assault and carrying a concealed weapon, and Cross was also arrested for assault based on an unsigned complaint. It was later realized

The Narragansett summer residence of Edith Hanan, who laughed in the face of the law. *Vintage postcard from the collection of the author.*

that the complaint was made in order to get Cross and his men out of the club. Once they were removed, unknown parties went into the club and secretly removed all traces of the gambling operation.

Cross was released due to the complaint against him being unsigned and went about his regular business as legal proceedings against Arnold were being carried out. Yet he was desperately besieged by the society women who had been in the gaming room that day to refrain from revealing their presence there. The embarrassment, they claimed, would forever alter their positions on the social ladder. One woman, however, gleamed rebelliously in the spotlight. Edith Hanan enjoyed telling newspaper reporters that she was present in the game room that evening. According to Edith, the whole ordeal was nothing more than a "joke" as far as she was concerned. The reports of the authorities, which had the high-society gamblers crying and fainting in fear for their reputations, were completely false, as Edith told it. Her crowd, she said, erupted into laughter when threatened by Cross and his men.

Edith was the wife of John Henry Hanan of New York, a shoe manufacturer and multimillionaire. Esteemed for his power and money, he was very influential in the development of Narragansett Pier as a wonderland for the rich. John had been married to another woman when he first met Edith. The two were engaged in an affair, and he had bestowed several thousand dollars' worth of jewelry on her. John was also courting another mistress, however, and he had promised the jewelry to her. When the other mistress took him to court for breach of promise, he sued Edith to get the jewelry back. The two finally overcame their differences and were married on April 16, 1903, just months after John's wife divorced him. He was Edith's third husband. Edith was well known in the society circles as being an elaborate hostess. The Hanans owned the largest gasoline-powered yacht in the world. Launched the year after their marriage, the 114-foot vessel was christened the *Edithia*.

Edith belittled Cross in the press, calling him a "country bumpkin." Her description of the raiders as being little more than a comedic act for the rich that evening led to the public consensus that Cross had gone overboard in his tirade against illegal gambling. The club owner was even let off the hook when the grand jury failed to indict him. The gambling taking place at Narragansett Pier continued. The games went on, as did the raids. The rich still enjoyed their summers just as they pleased, with little regard to laws they deemed laughable.

In 1920, the entire Hanan household became consumed by influenza and pneumonia. Edith died on January 11. Her son followed her in death eighteen days later, and her husband was laid to rest in August. The family's Narragansett villa, Shore Acres on Ocean Road, was eventually torn down. In time, the carefree laughter of the rich intertwined with the whirl of roulette wheels, the clatter of dice and shuffling of cards at the pier was silenced.

UNSAFE TRAVELS FOR DR. ALEXANDER BRIGGS
A Doctor and His Wife Are Held at Gunpoint

Dr. Alexander Burdick Briggs ventured to Florida each year for a rest. Never did he imagine that he and his wife would come close to being murdered there at the hands of a madman. The physician was born in Hopkinton on November 12, 1850, to Asa Sheldon Briggs and Mary (Burdick). Asa was the superintendent of a local woolen mill, and during the fall and winter months, he boarded area schoolteachers at his home.

Alexander graduated from Harvard Medical School in 1872 and immediately opened his own practice in Ashaway. On May 18, 1874, he marred Ella Maria Wells and went on to father two sons and a daughter. The couple made a practice of retiring to Daytona, Florida, each year when the Rhode Island weather turned cold. In February 1921, they were returning to their vacation home one evening after enjoying dinner at a Daytona restaurant. They hadn't ventured too far from the eatery when they saw a man up ahead approaching them. The man had a hat pulled down over his eyes and was very suspicious looking. The seventy-one-year-old doctor was certain it was his sixty-three-year-old brother, Leverett, attempting to pull a prank on them.

"Hands up!" the man ordered as he neared the couple's vehicle.

"Hands up nothing," Alexander replied, refusing to fall for his younger brother's joke.

Within seconds, there was a revolver pressed against Alexander's chest. Immediately, he realized this was no joke and quickly lifted his hands into the air. Ella jumped from the vehicle and started running down the road, screaming for help. The gunman pulled his weapon from Alexander's chest and aimed it in the direction of Ella. "Stop or I'll drop you!" he yelled. The sixty-eight-year-old woman didn't listen. She continued on, running down the road until she met up with an African American man riding a bicycle. She desperately explained to him what had just happened and that her husband was in danger. The man quickly

A resident of Ashaway, Dr. Alexander Briggs had some tough luck. *Vintage postcard courtesy of KarenLu LaPolice.*

followed her back to the vehicle. When the gunman saw them coming, he hit Alexander hard against the jaw and took off running. The couple was spared from being robbed of their money or shot; however, they ended their evening shaken up in a way they would never forget.

The following year, their travels found them in peril once again. On the morning of September 14, as they prepared to venture out of Wyoming toward Providence, their vehicle hit an obstruction in the road. Alexander broke several ribs and was taken to the home of Dr. Edwin Knerr to be attended to. Ella was transported to the hospital via ambulance, being more severely injured.

In 1923, Alexander decided to sell his practice and retire. His Ashaway business and all of his medical supplies were purchased by Dr. John Warden, who had recently been discharged from the army. Ella passed away in Ashaway on May 23, 1927, after suffering from a long illness. Alexander died at the home of his daughter, Donna Jackson, in Harris, Rhode Island. They were laid to rest in Oak Grove Cemetery.

Lawton Foster Cursed by a Heavy Club

Unfortunate Events in the Life of an Elderly Man

Most people go their entire lives without being on the giving or receiving end of a heavy club. But for Lawton Foster, such a weapon seemed to be almost a curse upon him. The son of Jonathan G. Foster and Patience (Kenyon), Lawton was born in Hopkinton in 1819. A farmer, he went on to marry Anne Worden and fathered two daughters and a son.

In September 1862, he enlisted as a private in Company G of the Twelfth Infantry of Rhode Island Volunteers, fighting the Civil War until being given an honorable discharge on July 29, 1863. While in the service, he was wounded and his eyesight became defective, earning him a pension of thirty dollars per month.

By 1900, his wife had died, and his children moved out on their own. He remained living in Hopkinton and had taken in a boarder to help out with the farm. To most, he was known as a respectable old gentleman, but that didn't prevent him from being hauled into court and charged with assault. Sixty-one-year-old Samuel Whitman sued Lawton in a jury trial in June 1900. Samuel claimed that he had been in the yard of his Hopkinton home

Though the town of Hopkinton often appeared to be calm, some residents just seemed to attract chaos. *Vintage photograph courtesy of Hope Greene Andrews.*

on July 5 of the previous year when Lawton appeared and stated that he intended to search Samuel's house for some reason or other. Samuel said he went into his house and shut the door, but soon after, Lawton came and broke the door down, striking Samuel with a four-foot-long club he gripped in his hand. Samuel alleged that Lawton's attack broke his arm and left him unable to work for three months.

Lawton denied this story and provided several witnesses to back him up. The defense argued that Lawton had not broken down Samuel's door, had not carried a club and had never struck the man with anything. One witness testified that around that time, Samuel had been intoxicated and bent down to pick up a jug of whiskey, but due to his drunken state, he had fallen down, breaking both his arm and the handle of the jug. Luckily, this witness saved Lawton from the consequences any real attack would have held, but nothing would save him from his next experience involving a club.

Nearly one year later, eighty-one-year-old Lawton went out onto his Canonchet farm to discover that his cattle were gone. He searched high and low for them, making his way around town until he spotted them in the field belonging to Thomas Edwards quite a distance away. Lawton began to drive the cattle back to his own farm, but suddenly a man jumped out from a hiding spot and began attacking Lawton with a club, bruising him severely.

Authorities were notified, and Lawton identified his attacker as Daniel Spencer. Daniel had been employed on Lawton's farm until he was let go from his position a short time earlier. It was believed that Daniel had driven the cattle from the farm as a way to get even with Lawton. Having had more than his share of experiences with the subject of heavy clubs, Lawton Foster died on a Monday afternoon in November 1907.

SHOOTINGS, MURDERS AND DRUNKEN BRAWLS

A House Notorious for Crime

Enoch Jerue looked up at Ollie Wright through bloodshot eyes. The checkerboard between them provided little barrier against what was about to happen. Ollie wasn't playing fairly, according to Enoch. But Ollie saw it the other way around. So far, it had been just another regular Saturday night for the tavern-loving locals of Hope Valley in the year 1909. Twenty-eight-year-old Enoch and his wife's three brothers—twenty-nine-year-old Osworth, "Ollie"; twenty-four-year-old Thomas; and eighteen-year-old Frederick—had spent a good part of the evening getting drunk at a Wyoming saloon before coming back to Enoch's house for a friendly game of checkers.

When inebriation began to overwhelm sportsmanship, Enoch ended the game by ordering the trio of brothers out of his house. They obligingly left, but a few minutes later, Ollie returned and busted down the door with an axe. If he wanted to play rough, Enoch was ready. He reached over and grabbed his shotgun, aiming it at his brother-in-law. Enoch's wife, Dora, a twenty-seven-year-old dressmaker, tried to calm the situation. After all, the couple's seven-year-old daughter, Nellie, was trying to sleep in another room. She explained to her brother Ollie that it was best if he just went away, as Enoch was very upset over the checker game. Ollie turned and left, making his way down the small hill and reaching the road before a gunshot rang out. Ollie leapt in pain as a bullet sank itself into his left foot. A local doctor cleaned and dressed the wound, but he thought it best that Ollie go on to Rhode Island Hospital to have it checked out there. Enoch was arrested and arraigned two days later before being held on a $1,000 bond.

Although the houses in Hope Valley were usually picturesque, it was surprising what sometimes occurred inside them. *Vintage photograph courtesy of Hope Greene Andrews.*

The Jerue property didn't gain its reputation for craziness that night. The events there on that cold evening of March 20 were merely added to the list of strange occurrences that had taken place in that location over the years. In 1885, the property was owned by Dennison S. Healy, who liked his liquor a little too much, as did his much younger wife, Elizabeth. Neighbors often heard them engaged in loud, drunken bouts. Then one beautiful summer day, Elizabeth shot and killed him in the kitchen.

Prior to that, it is said that a married woman by the name of Molly lived there. The story varies; some say Molly killed her husband and threw his body in the pond out back, while others say it was Molly who was killed by her spouse and disposed of in the pond. Either way, Molly Pond is said to be named for this fatal event.

The Jerue/Healy place was located not far from Pine Grove Cemetery. A short walk from the back of the property leads one to Molly Pond. Only foundations remain today, wrapped in a tangle of vines and overgrown bushes. The former site of shootings, murder and drunken brawls, it garners no present-day attention.

Saloon Owner Welcome Fidler Earns Quite a Reputation

Numerous Raids Can't Stop Man from a Lifetime of Illegal Activity

A thorough history of Woodville could hardly be written without mentioning the name Welcome Fidler. A somewhat infamous character, he was as well known to the local preachers as he was to the alcoholics and the Rhode Island court system.

Born in 1863 to Edward Fidler and Adelia (Baggs), he and two older sisters would be the only children of the six born to his parents to survive past the age of six. Welcome married Jennie Tibbetts in 1885 and fathered three children: Thomas, Jennie and another who died young. He settled on the Richmond side of Woodville and worked as a carriage manufacturer in Wood River Junction for several years before becoming a "merchant," though that word held different meanings to different people. Occasionally, Welcome's "clerks" lived at his house with him and his family.

The year 1895 brought one of Welcome's first forays into the court. After an argument with his uncle Albert Baggs over the ownership of a tract of land in Woodville, he was sued for allegedly assaulting the sixty-six-year-old man. The following year, another piece of Woodville land, which had been jointly inherited by Welcome and his two sisters upon their mother's death in 1892, was sold at public auction by the Hopkinton collector of taxes.

Welcome's father, Edward Fidler, owned a grocery store in the village and also held the position of postmaster at Richmond Switch. When he passed away in 1904, his will named Welcome as executor, and properties were left to an assortment of family members. By this time, Welcome had already garnered a reputation for maintaining a "rum hole." In the spring of 1901, upon the complaint of Reverend Eric Lindh, Welcome was charged with the sale and possession of illegal alcohol. The winter before, two young men who worked for the Anti-Saloon League had been sent to visit Welcome's "store" undercover. They described entering the dwelling through a room that looked like a tavern, with bottles baring labels such as "Sherry" and "Hermitage" on the shelves. One of the men testified that he ordered a whiskey while the other ordered wine, and they bought a half-pint of whiskey to take home with them.

Welcome took the stand, stating that although he had "many occupations," he did not run a saloon, and the bottles the two men saw on the shelves were the products of a "bottling establishment" he owned. He went on to say that he and his friend James Thurman were the only people present when the two detectives entered the building and that one of them claimed to be a photographer peddling his wares. As that man showed his photos, he said, the other dropped comfortably into an armchair.

Within the beauty of Woodville stood a structure that was like a magnet for inebriates. *Vintage photograph from the collection of the author.*

Welcome said one of them picked up a bottle of whiskey, which was for his own personal enjoyment, and asked if he could have a drink. He stated that he obliged and served both men. Later, he said, he offered them both some of his homemade grape wine. Aside from those two bottles, Welcome testified, the only other alcohol in the place was a half-flask of brandy he had procured for his father, who was sick. He stated that after the two men left, he noticed the flask was missing. He and Mr. Thurman went in pursuit of the men, catching up with them at the train station, where a brawl ensued. When the detectives refused to relinquish the bottle, which was hidden in a coat pocket, a ruckus that included hair pulling and choking took place and caused the flask to open and the brandy to spill out of the coat.

James Thurman testified on behalf of Welcome, as did Charles Babcock, an employee of Welcome who stated that Edward Fidler had requested that he fetch a bottle of brandy from his son. The two detectives did not impress many of the jury members, correcting the grammar of Welcome's attorney and flaunting their Brown University educations. In the end, the jury could not come to an agreement about whether Welcome was guilty of the charges. This was the not the last time, however, that he would be hauled into court, accused of maintaining a saloon and illegally selling alcohol.

Perhaps Jennie had gotten tired of it all a few years later when she filed for a legal separation. She was granted a release from her husband's bed and board and awarded alimony of eight dollars per week. She was also given custody of the couple's two living children. Welcome fought the order of the court, accusing Jennie of committing adultery. The court determined that there was no evidence of adultery and ruled that the motion for alimony remain in full force.

In 1906, Welcome Fidler's seventeen-year-old son, Thomas, petitioned for a guardian over his share of his grandfather's estate. He chose his mother, much to Welcome's dismay. That same year, the home Welcome and Jennie had shared in Woodville before their separation went up for public auction when the mortgage went unpaid. Having never made any of his obligatory alimony payments, Welcome appealed to the court the following summer for a divorce and an end to the alimony order. Jennie contested this and won. The case of *Fidler v. Fidler* had been in the court for quite some time now due to Welcome's refusal to allot money to his wife, and her attorney wanted him held in contempt of court.

No sooner had the hearing on this matter been rescheduled for another time than, that same day, Jennie was called to the stand to defend herself in the *Kenyon v. Fidler* suit. Welcome's sister Lydia was suing Jennie for trespass and asked for her removal from the home where she was living. The tenement house where Jennie had been residing since the separation had been left to Lydia and Welcome upon their mother's death. Jennie had been told to get out nearly a year earlier. Believing the property was still in her husband's name, she refused to leave, even when presented with a notice from the police sergeant. Welcome suddenly informed the court that he had sold his interest in the property to Peter Palmer quite some time ago. Jennie's attorney argued that, in light of Welcome's refusal to pay alimony, Jennie had no money to relocate. The jury, however, ruled that she must vacate the house. This ejectment wasn't enough to make Welcome happy. He appealed to the court to reverse the decision of the Hopkinton Probate Court, which had made Jennie the guardian of son Thomas's property. This appeal was denied.

Once again, things didn't go the way Welcome wanted them to the following year when the R.L. Rose Company of Providence sued him over three parcels of land in Woodville that had been conveyed to him by his father. The land soon ended up in a sheriff's sale. Where Welcome was concerned, there always seemed to be something for people to talk about. No matter how many times he appeared before the court, it would not allow him to sever his marriage to the wife who had left him. And anyone would have been hard-pressed, during this time period, to find a local newspaper article concerning crimes involving alcohol that did not mention Welcome Fidler. It was common for such criminals to admit they had imbibed in a few drinks at Fidler's before committing their illegal acts. He was regularly arrested, released, raided and represented by attorneys who made him out to be the perpetual victim of untruths. When he was charged with criminally assaulting his son around 1908, he decided to cut his ties to Woodville, where he had lost nearly everything he had, and relocate to Mystic.

This could have been Welcome's chance to turn over a new leaf. He settled into a home on Pearl Street and employed a live-in housekeeper. Then he opened the Mystic Lunch & Pool Room. But in September 1909, the business was raided, and police found one hundred bottles of beer in iceboxes that were in plain view and a large quantity of whiskey in pint and half-pint bottles. Welcome acted shocked by his arrest. Unable to furnish bonds, he was transported to the jail in Groton. With legal representation, Welcome was released from his incarceration, but in 1915, his place was raided again, and he was taken into custody after a large quantity of alcohol, mostly whiskey, was discovered. Released once more, he relocated to New Bedford. The husband and father who had once laid claim to so many stretches of Woodville land was now renting a place on Purchase Street, where he lived alone with his maid and worked as a mechanic in a cotton mill.

Jennie moved with her son to Westerly and passed away in 1954. Welcome spent the rest of his life at the Purchase Street rental, and apparently as he aged, his desire for the wild life declined. It's not known when he died or if he ever consented to make those alimony payments to the woman from whom he was legally separated. However, in 1930, he is recorded as finally being a "divorced" man.

RUM SELLERS AND GIN DEALERS
Raids Were Once a Common Occurrence

Despite angering lawmakers and the temperance crowds, the rum sellers and gin dealers of Washington County never found themselves at a loss for business. As long as there were drinkers, there were people around to provide the drink, and quite regularly, there was a raid going on somewhere.

Forty-six-year-old Charles Brown, who lived on the turnpike just a short distance from Canonchet, had spent part of the summer of 1907 behind bars. Brown had been caught illegally selling alcohol, and the stint in jail might have reformed some people, but not Brown. It was the night

Amos Dawley of Wyoming had one of the most popular taverns in Washington County. *Vintage postcard courtesy of Hope Greene Andrews.*

before Thanksgiving when the police showed up at his home once again after receiving a tip that Brown was still in the business of intoxicating the locals. Armed with a search warrant, two officers watched Brown through a window before making their entrance. There he stood, pouring alcohol from a bottle into a tumbler for a gentleman who waited for his drink. The officers rushed into the house and grabbed for the bottle. Brown tried to throw it aside, but one of the officers got ahold of it first and determined that it contained whiskey. The officer looked at the man with the tumbler and asked him what was in it. "That's none of your business," the man replied as he attempted to put the tumbler in his shirt pocket and accidentally spilled it all over himself. The officers searched the house, locating a small quantity of whiskey. In the cellar, they discovered a two-gallon jug of wine. The search continued outside, where one of the officers noticed a suspicious-looking bag underneath the porch. It was out of reach and accessible only through a window in the cellar. Once they pulled it out, the officers found that it contained a one-gallon jug nearly filled with more whiskey.

If anyone expected a raid such as this to set Brown on a straight course, they were wrong. Two days before Christmas, the police were again at the Brown property. This time, they seized five bottles of alcohol and a barrel containing about nineteen gallons of wine. Though Brown was a wood dealer by trade, his side job and the raids it caused must have certainly made life interesting for those he lived with—his younger brother, their teenage sister and their elderly widowed mother.

Another local raid just before Thanksgiving 1907 occurred after a mass of intoxicated men began roaming the streets of Hopkinton and ruining the afternoon for several residents. Everyone noticed that they seemed to be coming from the vicinity of Charles Moore's house. Just before dark, the troubled Thomas Champlin was reeling about town, bleeding from a wound on his head and angrily declaring that he had just been in a fight at Moore's residence. Securing a gun, Champlin announced that he was going to return to Moore's and "shoot up the house." A few locals were able calm Champlin down while another summoned police. When an officer arrived, Champlin told him about being beat up while he was at Moore's, and the officer obtained a search warrant before going on to the site of the row. By the time he arrived and explained that he was there to search the premises for illegal alcohol, Moore had taken off. The woman who answered the door assured the officer that there was no alcohol on the property.

Armed with the warrant, the officer began his search anyway. Hidden in a trunk, he discovered a bottle partly filled with wine. The woman told the officer it was hers. He also located a pint of whiskey. Another discovery was made beneath a loose floorboard, where a crawl space revealed a quart-sized bottle two-thirds filled with whiskey and a drinking glass set beside it. As a woman was involved, gossip flew just as it had earlier that year when, in July, a local woman was arrested for illegally selling intoxicating drink. Kate Larose, who lived near the cranberry bog in Richmond, was hauled off to jail one morning on the strength of two warrants.

Reputation didn't seem to make much of a difference when it came to who was peddling intoxicants. The rum-hole owners were doing it, but so were many soft-spoken, respectable citizens. During the summer of 1924, the special liquor constable teamed up with several other men to raid the home of Walter Cekala, who lived on Mechanic Street in Hope Valley. The thirty-one-year-old Polish immigrant kept a meat market and may have been providing more than cold cuts to local residents. The authorities discovered and seized twenty-eight bottles of alcohol on the property.

ELDERLY MARY RICH DISAPPEARS WHILE DELIVERING EGGS

A Ninety-Four-Year-Old Woman Goes Missing in the Snowy Woods

French Canadian Mary Rich wrapped her heavy double scotch plaid shawl around her shoulders, filled her egg basket and headed off to make deliveries. The ninety-four-year-old Charlestown woman regularly supplied nearby homes and stores with the eggs her chickens provided on her farm, known as the "George Ammons place." Rich had been married three times, and her current husband, William, who worked as a woodchopper, was forty-three years her junior. Despite her advanced age, Rich was in full control of her faculties and maintained a very active life. She left the house early in the afternoon that day of February 5, 1904. The air was cold, and her steps took her across snow-covered ground. George Chaffee and Frank Burdick were chopping wood on a hill near the Pawcatuck River later that day when Rich approached them. She appeared to be troubled and began talking to the two men in her native French language, which they were unable to understand. Unsuccessful in her attempts to communicate what the trouble was, she finally went on her way.

When night came and Rich still hadn't returned home, her husband became concerned. He began to search for her, inquiring of all the

Horseshoe Falls in the village of Shannock, where the elderly Mary Rich seemingly disappeared. *Vintage postcard courtesy of KarenLu LaPolice.*

neighbors whether they had seen her. Only Chaffee and Burdick replied in the affirmative. The strange disappearance had hundreds of men and boys gathered together the following day. They scoured the woods, forcing their way through dense thickets and enduring the bitter New England weather in hopes of locating Mrs. Rich alive. Soon, they discovered her egg basket and walking cane lying beside a cart path in the woods. Talk made its way around town; perhaps she had fallen somewhere and frozen to death, or maybe she was lost. Still others thought the entire situation hinted at foul play. Finally, the talk died down. The days passed, then weeks, months and years. William Rich moved away from the farm, and the disappearance of his wife remained unsolved. Then, on November 3, 1907, twenty-three-year-old Dallas Robert Woodmansee was walking through the woods when he stumbled upon a body in a swamp on the farm belonging to Chaffee, about three and a half miles from Rich's former home. The body was mostly skeletonized and beneath a two-foot-thick layer of dead leaves. Recalling that a woman had disappeared three years earlier, authorities called in Dr. John Welcome Saunders and Rich's grandson to see if they could identify the body. Both parties knew what Rich had been wearing when she left the house that cold winter day and were able to identify the body as hers by the remnants of the plaid shawl wrapped around the shoulders and the cloth-top shoes covered with rubbers.

There were no signs of foul play in the death of Mary Rich. And no one would ever know what her quandary had been on that day when she desperately tried to gain the assistance of two men who didn't understand French.

THOMAS SEGAR AND HIS DAUGHTER'S SUITOR COME TO BLOWS
Threats and a Physical Altercation Disrupt Romance

Sometimes the blossom of love is pinched away, leaving a destiny decided by the choices of others instead of fate itself. Thomas Browning Segar was a well-do-to and highly respected merchant in Hopkinton. He and his wife, Georgiana (Randall), had two children: Thomas, born in 1866, and Dora Lee, born in 1876. Dora was a charming girl who grew into a beautiful young lady with an energetic wit and captivating personality. The boys of Hopkinton were drawn to Dora, but none so much as Samuel Orcelus

Barber. The son of Jared George Barber and Artemissa (Burdick), Samuel was a simple country boy who wanted little more than to have Dora on his arm. The feeling was mutual. Seventeen-year-old Dora and twenty-four-year-old Samuel were in love, and everyone in town knew it.

In the fall of 1893, Dora was finishing her last year at the prestigious Friends School in Providence when she met a male student who became taken with her. Dora was friendly with the boy, but the keeper of her heart was back in Hope Valley. This was no deterrent to the boy, however. He contacted her parents and asked if he might visit their home for the purpose of calling on Dora. Thomas liked what he learned about this suitor, especially the fact that he was to inherit $100,000 when he turned twenty-one. He readily gave permission for the boy to call on his daughter. During his visit, Thomas and Georgiana were completely smitten with him. It was quickly decided that this was the boy they wanted to court Dora and that Samuel Barber was no longer welcome at their home.

Dora strongly refused to be separated from Samuel and informed her mother of such. The argument grew so heated that Georgiana grabbed a yardstick and began to hit Dora with it. Fleeing from her home, the teenage girl ran to a neighbor's house for protection. The young lovers began to meet on the sly, stealing quick moments whenever time and circumstance allowed. They knew they had to be careful, but unfortunately they weren't careful enough. During one secret rendezvous, Georgiana came upon them. She began to give a loud, lengthy lecture about how the two of them were not ever going to be together again. When they refused to agree to her demands, she reached down to scoop up mud, dirt and stones, with which she forcefully pelted them. Dora and Samuel quickly ran from the scene, and Georgiana went home. Josiah Palmer, who lived nearby and had witnessed the whole assault, took his son outside to help him collect the stones in case Dora and Samuel needed evidence of the attack. Townspeople were divided over the whole affair. There were those who felt Thomas and his wife were right in choosing the best partner for their daughter, and then there were those who felt the young couple should simply be left alone.

Not long after this incident, residents gathered at the depot one day to await the scheduled train. It was transporting the Plainville Brass band, which was to give a performance in Hope Valley. Among the crowd were Dora and Samuel. They were thoroughly enjoying the anticipation until Thomas arrived and saw them together. He approached them and angrily demanded an explanation of why they were in each other's company when he had forbidden it. The attention of the crowd veered away from thoughts

MAYHEM

Those who lived in Hope Valley found themselves divided when it came to the forbidden love affair between Dora Segar and Samuel Barber. *Vintage photograph courtesy of Hope Greene Andrews.*

of music and rested on the loud argument taking place between Thomas, Dora and Samuel. Suddenly, Thomas reached out and punched Samuel in the face. When the boy offered no retaliation, Thomas began to slap him across the face repeatedly. Samuel tried to walk away, but Thomas chased after him and again tried to physically instigate a brawl. As the stunned crowd watched, Dora jumped between the two men. She looked up at her father and gave him a stinging slap across his cheek. She began yelling, and Thomas ordered her to calm down. When she refused, he picked her up and carried her home. She would no longer be allowed to leave the house.

The following evening, a calm, spring night in 1894, Dora snuck out of her temporary prison and joined the man she loved, who was waiting for her outside. With their hearts racing, they quickly made their way down Spring Street to the depot, where Dora hid in the darkness behind a pile of railroad ties while Samuel went home to get his horse and buggy. Their plan was to escape to New Jersey, where they could live their lives together in peace. It took them an hour to reach Westerly, where they abandoned the horse and wagon and boarded the train to New London. Later, as they impatiently waited for their boat's departure, Dora became violently sick. Samuel rented

67

a room at a nearby hotel and took her there to lie down. Gossip spread like wildfire through Hope Valley concerning the alleged secret elopement of Dora Segar and Samuel Barber. Thomas raged as he scoured towns near and far in search of his disobedient daughter. By Saturday morning, he had gathered enough information to determine the location of the couple. He entered the hotel room where Dora still lay ill. He grabbed her and brought her back to Hope Valley, where she was warned to not ever go near Samuel again.

On the afternoon of May 22, 1897, Dora Lee was dressed in a heavy white satin gown and carrying a large bouquet of lilies of the valley as she walked down the aisle on the arm of her father. At the opposite side of the church, her soon-to-be-husband waited. His name was Albert N. Chappell. It is not known whether this was the man with whom Dora's parents had been so smitten, but it was someone Thomas approved of, someone other than Samuel Barber. The reception was held at Thomas's home, and no expense was spared. There was a caterer, exquisite floral arrangements and costly gifts. The couple later boarded the boat for New York, where they would go on to Albert's father's house in Virginia for their honeymoon. Dora's mother was not at the wedding. Georgiana had passed away in April 1896. While nursing Dora through a dangerous bout of scarlet fever, she had caught the disease herself and succumbed to it.

The Chappells settled in Westerly, where Albert was employed as a railroad station assistant. He would later go on to become a dentist. By 1905, they were divorced. Dora rented a room at Agnes Riley's boardinghouse in Providence and worked as an instructor for a local sewing machine company. Samuel Barber was living happily with his wife and three children in Hopkinton. He had married a French Canadian girl named Corinne Mignault in 1896 and was working successfully as a house carpenter. In 1911, he moved his family to Westerly, where he had gained a position as boss carpenter for Isaac Sherman. On November 16, 1916, he had just finished a day's work in Pawcatuck and was walking home when he decided to take a shortcut. It was about 4:30 p.m. when he stepped onto the train tracks that spanned the bridge over the Pawcatuck River just west of the station. The engineer of the Knickerbocker Express, which had just come around the curve at over fifty miles an hour, was horrified to see someone right in front of him on the tracks. He blew the whistle and applied the brakes, but it was no use. Samuel was struck with great force, fracturing his skull and breaking his left arm, left collarbone and several ribs on both sides of his body.

Samuel was hurled eighty feet away from where he was struck, catapulting into the cement abutment and then falling into the water below. A man named Albert Rodman, who had witnessed the accident, rushed to the riverbank and waded in. He pulled Samuel's body ashore, but it was obvious he was dead. A coroner's report later stated that his lungs were filled with water and that his ultimate cause of death was drowning. He was forty-seven years old and laid to rest in Rockville Cemetery. Dora had moved to California by that time and remarried. She and her husband, a school janitor, had a one-year-old child.

KATE SPRAGUE, A WIFE TURNED HOSTAGE
Wealthy Business Owner Transforms Matrimony into a Nightmare

For many women in the 1800s, life itself was like a corset—restraining and simply endured, reflective only of what was deemed proper and acceptable. Yet every now and then, a woman would cut the strings, freeing herself to take her first long and uninterrupted breath. Such women, who fished for their dignity in the depths of expectation, were usually looked down on by society. Yet those women are the ones for whom history applauds.

Catherine Jane Chase was born on August 13, 1840, to Salmon Portland Chase and Eliza Ann Smith. She was named for Salmon's first wife, Catherine Jane Garniss, who had died one year into the marriage. Salmon's first child had also been named Catherine Jane; however, she passed away at the age of five, just three months before his first child with Eliza was born.

By the age of five, Catherine, who was fondly called "Kate," had lost three sisters and her mother. Salmon moved his own two sisters into the house to help him care for Kate. In 1846, Salmon married his third wife, Sara Bella Dunlop Ludlow. Two children were born of the union, one of whom was a daughter who did not survive. By the time she was nine years old, Kate had been sent away to Miss Haines's boarding school in New York City. While there, she received a letter from her father informing her that her stepmother, Sara, had died. If the deep loss with which she was constantly confronted was not enough to weigh heavy on a little girl's mind, her father's letters undoubtedly added to the burden. In them, he rambled on about the shadow of death that seemed to surround them and that, because of it, he did not expect to live long. Hoping to extend his daughter's life, he warned her to be constantly aware of the dangers all around her. He urged her to maintain the morals of a saint and to improve anything about herself that did not reach the level of perfection.

At fourteen, Kate was switched to a different boarding school, this one located in Pennsylvania. The following year, she returned home. Salmon would soon be elected governor of Ohio. Whether political or personal, everything going on in his life was discussed with Kate. Extremely intelligent for her age, she often provided advice to her father, which he took into careful consideration. By the time she had reached her late teens, Kate was occupying positions on several political committees, where her education and confidence allowed her to be an outspoken participant. The men who filled the other seats did not like the situation at all. And while the local men disliked Kate, the local women despised her. A girl publicly exhibiting her intelligence and stepping onto grounds reserved for men was not acceptable.

In 1861, Salmon was named secretary of the treasury, and he moved his daughter and himself to Washington, D.C. There, Kate assisted her father in the world of politics, took care of the household chores and hosted elegant parties, which all the high-ranking politicians attended. Abraham Lincoln was an acquaintance of Salmon's, and Mrs. Lincoln's opinion of Kate was not unlike that of other women. It was rumored that Mary harbored such jealousy toward the young girl that she maintained a distance between Kate and Abe. However, she had nothing to worry about. Kate's heart had already been stolen by that time. While in Ohio to attend the dedication of a monument honoring Oliver Hazard Perry, she met William Sprague. At thirty years old, he was ten years Kate's elder. The son of Amasa Sprague and Fanny Morgan of Cranston, he was known far and wide as Rhode Island's "Boy Wonder." The year before, he had been elected governor, despite the fact that he had no experience in politics. There were whispers of bribery and dirty dealing, and it was alleged that he had spent over $100,000 to buy the position. There was little that he couldn't buy if he wanted to. His grandfather had built one of the first cotton mills in the state. His father and uncles turned the business into a financial empire, forming the A&W Sprague Company and gaining ownership of mills across the country.

When William was twelve years old, his father was found murdered not far from their Cranston home. It was believed that his powerful influence and opposition to alcohol had riled some feathers. A man named John Gordon was hanged for the crime. William's uncle inherited the A&W Sprague Company, and when he died fourteen years later, the twenty-six-year-old William became the new owner. William had always liked being in charge of things. At the age of sixteen, he had joined the Providence Marine Artillery, and during his courtship with Kate, he was heading the First Rhode Island Regiment. However, just as women did not like Kate, men were not fond of William. After just three months under his leadership, the recruits of the First Regiment left his camp and went home. Wild with anger, he accused them of cowardice and sent for new troops. When none arrived, he, too, returned home.

During his absence, letters passed between William and Kate. His flowery prose was an attempt to titillate her with hues of egotism as he assured her that he was well aware of her fondness for him. Then, without obvious cause, his letters stopped coming. William had become interested in another woman, Mary Eliza Viall of Providence. His interest waned when Viall told him he was going to be a father. Deciding it was time to cut his ties there, he resumed his relationship with Kate.

Despite his lack of experience, William was reelected governor in 1861 and 1862. The following year, he was elected senator. Kate received a marriage proposal and went to meet the prosperous family she would soon become a part of. During that first visit, she and William became engaged in an argument that threw a veil of discomfort over the entire party. Kate later penned a letter to Fanny, apologizing for the disruption. William thanked Kate for the gesture, informing her that since the argument had been all her fault, apologizing for her exhibition of "strange conduct" had been the right thing to do.

William's wedding gift to his new bride was a jeweled tiara, and for some reason, he felt the need to inform her of its cost. This was concerning to her—if not for the breach of etiquette, then for the fact that he tossed away money so frivolously. On November 12, 1863, Kate became Mrs. William Sprague. The lavish wedding was held in Washington, with President Lincoln among the many guests. But no air of fantasy blinded Kate. She was already desperately hoping that once they settled into married life, William would change his ways and act like a husband. Those who knew him well blamed his rude and brash behavior on low self-confidence. Often insensitive, he refused to explain his thoughts or actions to anyone. Viall once described him as "cloaking himself in a veil of mystery."

Kate did not want a mystery. She wanted a husband. However, any knowledge of what was happening in William's life, heart or mind was not offered to her. He was rarely home, leaving her alone while he continued to live the life of a bachelor. When she complained to him, he sent her a letter explaining that he had many responsibilities and that he hoped she did not intend to be "an additional burden" on his time. She tried to be understanding, asking about the facets of his business in hopes that she could be of some assistance. However, he told her that she had no place in his business, and he had no desire to discuss things that did not concern her.

Kate confided to her friends that William's family was often rude to her, and he did nothing to curb their offensive behaviors. While they had once been deemed "a brilliant match," the differences between William and Kate were becoming obvious to everyone. Kate discovered a letter that William had written to a male employee, droning on and on about the incompatibilities between him and his wife. While he felt free to discuss such personal matters, Kate was forbidden to talk about their union with anyone. After once learning that she had confided in her father after a matrimonial argument, William penned a letter to her, stating that, "as a special favor" this one time, he would forgive her for such a betrayal. While Kate's vision of her husband was darkening, so was that held by the public. No longer did everyone so quickly adhere to the attractions William Sprague dangled in front of them. His etiquette was dramatic and insincere, and his image was an overinflated façade. It was as if he desperately sought to project an existence coveted by all. Kate was given the finest clothing and jewelry. She was encouraged to plan and host the most luxurious balls imaginable. She had the life all women dreamed of in the eyes of those who did not know the emptiness of her existence. The fineries were merely props in the picture that William wanted the world to see.

In 1866, Kate gave birth to the couple's first child, Willie. Three years later, daughter Ethel was born, and in 1872, daughter Katherine arrived. With motherhood, Kate's responsibilities increased, along with her desperation to see a change in her husband. William's self-absorption, however, grew to new heights. He blew up his ego for anyone who would watch, strolling through his factories as if he walked on air. He purchased a million-dollar farmhouse standing on four hundred acres of land in Narragansett—which he named Canonchet, after an Indian chief—and ordered the house renovated into a three-story, sixty-three-room mansion to rival anything about which the wealthy of Newport could brag. Kate was given the job of decorating the new residence. She threw herself into the project as if it were a form of therapy. Filling up the emptiness of the new house, she hung up pictures to brighten dark rooms and put things where there had been nothing before to reduce the echoes of hollowness.

William was rarely around, though he occasionally required his wife to accompany him to his family's home for a visit. She despised the city and the discomfort of sitting among people with whom she clearly had nothing in common. But this marriage was hers, for better or worse, even when the public gossips knew more about her husband's life than she did. She heard the talk of his affairs and his complaints about the marriage, and if she dared confront him about any of it, he would conveniently lay the blame on her. Humiliation burned inside her like fire. But respectable women of that time did not walk away from their husbands. There was no such thing as being courageous enough to leave an abusive union. Women were expected to be courageous enough to stay. What had once been love had transformed into something ugly and painful. William had become Kate's cross to bear. Kate had become just another of William's holdings over which he had complete control. While he continued to cast about his money for all to see, he began refusing to allow Kate any money for her own use. Reddened with embarrassment, she would plead with him for money, and he made it a point to give his refusal in the presence of an audience.

In the fall of 1873, when Kate gave birth to their fourth child, a girl she named Portia, she and William had been living apart for several months. William's businesses were now failing due to mismanagement, and his reputation was worth little more than fodder for the newspapers. The riches he cared about so deeply were slipping through his fingers like sand, and banks were refusing to provide him with loans or credit as he was deemed to be too much of a financial risk. Wishing to remove herself from the public eye, Kate packed up her children and went on an extended trip to Europe. Her husband kept in touch. "You know I am fond of the ladies and you must not blame me for indulging in that fondness," he wrote to her in one letter. She responded by telling him that she no longer cared whether he chose to commit adultery and that he was free to do whatever he wanted. William was extremely upset by her lack of jealousy.

Financially, Kate was struggling, but she swore she would never again beg her husband for a dime. She devoted herself to raising their children as best as she could, directing much attention to daughter "Kitty," who was developmentally delayed. Eventually, she decided to return to Canonchet, but just like before, she found she simply could not endure her invisibility in the eyes of her husband and the embarrassing gossip that his behavior caused. She packed up her children and left again, telling newspaper reporters, "His dissolute life and dissipated habits long ago interrupted our marital relations. I have striven through untold humiliation and pain to hide from the world the true condition of a miserable domestic life, for my children's sakes." She went on to describe her husband as unreliable in business and unmanly in his personal life: "He comes in like a ghost in the middle of the night and at the most unreasonable hours, then hurries away in the same manner." She stated that he had allowed no financial support for her or the children for several months and refused to pay any bills. She accused him of neglect, indecency and casting financial hardship on her in order to assert his authority. When the newspaper hit the stands, William got a taste of the embarrassment he had been casting over his wife for so many years. He was enraged.

A few days later, Kate obtained a divorce attorney. With his cocky air, William informed Kate that if she divorced him, he would take the children away from her. With such a threat thrown into the ring, Kate's attorney advised her to withdraw from divorce proceedings. She agreed but remained living at her father's residence, Edgewood, and made it clear that she was not William Sprague's wife but his unwilling hostage. She went to the newspapers again:

> *I bore with meekness the unmanly sneers and reproaches showered upon me, not responding save when my children's relations to me were touched upon. These years of my life have been a constant drag upon me. I have striven to stand between my husband's wrongdoing and the public. I have done it for the sake of our children, not for any affection that existed between us, for there has been none for years.*

William exploded when he read her reports. He accused her of attempting to poison the children's minds against him and demanded that she turn over custody of them to him. Kate immediately consulted her attorney and was informed that, in Rhode Island, the father of minor children maintained legal rights over them. William took the children and transported them back to Canonchet. Being with William was unbearable, but being without her children was unthinkable. Kate returned to Canonchet as well. At once, William tightened his grip on his wife's freedom, publicly announcing that it was in her best interest, as she had become mentally unbalanced. When they were alone, he would remind her again and again that if she left him, she would be forfeiting her life as a mother.

Kate's desperation grew until she could take no more. One night while William slept, she took the children and fled from the home. With the help of her lawyer, she later attempted to gain possession of personal items in the home, such as sentimental items she'd inherited from her father. William, however, claimed that the contents of the house included nothing of hers. Kate again filed for divorce on the grounds of adultery and extreme cruelty. She asked for custody of the children as well as alimony.

William wasn't going to let his wife simply walk away. He decided to countersue for divorce, claiming that Kate had committed adultery, squandered his property and deserted him. With William using every delay tactic he could find, the court proceedings went on for over a year. Finally, in May 1882, Kate was granted her freedom and given custody of the children. Pretending to be unscathed, William began bragging of his future plans in the world of politics. One reporter responded to this news by stating, "To elect William Sprague again as governor is to encourage robbery, cheating and repudiation." Another reporter called him "a defiant bankrupt who has passed years and years in preventing his creditors from being paid." Nothing that was being said could puncture his ego or force him to see what a mess his life had become. Less than a year after the divorce, he married again and eventually moved to Paris. He died there of meningitis at the age of eighty-four in 1915.

Kate returned to Edgewood with her children. Poverty-stricken, she turned her father's estate into a farm and struggled to survive on the sale of eggs, vegetables, milk and butter, which she peddled door to door at local hotels. The highly intelligent, lively young girl filled with hope and promise had become a poor, aged farmer. The jewels were gone, along with the ball gowns and mansions. The lavish parties were over, and the awe-stricken glances of those who had once coveted her life were no more. She would now forever be a woman with fingers pointed at her in disgrace, a woman who had committed the sin of divorce. It was not until after her death in 1899, at the age of fifty-nine, that the dark veil was pulled off the memory of Kate Sprague. People began to understand that she had left women everywhere an inheritance. The light inside of her that she had fought to keep burning continued to burn after her life was over. What she represented was the embodiment of a woman who chose to give up nearly everything she had in order to hold on to one thing: her dignity.

PART II

MURDER

SUSPECT IN MURDER OF LAURA REGESTER IS FOUND

Suspected Killer of a Providence Woman Is Located for Questioning

When police arrived at the Hope Valley farm where Ernest Allen was employed, he spoke with them willingly. Certainly, he implied, he wanted to do everything he could to help them discover who had killed his ex-wife. Charles Douglas of Providence also cooperated with police. The dead woman was his fiancée, and he would obviously do whatever was necessary to help them in their investigation. Systematically, they and other men were arrested and questioned about the brutal murder of Laura E. Regester.

Laura was a beautiful twenty-five-year-old woman who lived in Cranston with her widowed father, Charles William Regester, an employee of the Gorham Company. Her mother, Harriet (Oldale), had died when Laura was just five years old. Following her divorce from Ernest, Laura had returned to her father's home on Pleasant Street, where she kept house for him. At 7:40 p.m. on May 10, 1909, Laura left her father's residence and boarded a public car, which took her to her destination of Public Street. There, she did a fitting with the dressmaker she had hired to create her wedding gown. She left the shop at 9:45 p.m., stating that she was going to get on the 10:20 p.m. public car to go home. Witnesses saw her get off the car that evening at

Residents of Hopkinton were shocked to learn that a cold-blooded killer may have been in town. *Vintage photograph courtesy of Hope Greene Andrews.*

the cemetery, not far from her father's home. But no one ever saw her alive again, at least no one who would admit to it. Around midnight, those who lived in the vicinity of the cemetery heard a scream.

The following day, at 7:15 a.m., Joseph Rosen, an employee of the Sherwood Ice Company in Providence, was walking past the Sons of Israel Jewish cemetery located on Reservoir Avenue, next door to the ice company, when he came upon a shocking sight. He quickly summoned his foreman, who immediately sent for police. The body of a young woman lay beaten and mutilated within the cemetery grounds. Her eyes, nose and forehead showed evidence of vicious blows to the head. Bruises and the imprints of finger marks on her neck indicated strangulation, which was done with such force that bones were broken on both sides of her neck. Her torso and limbs had been grotesquely cut and mutilated, and her torn, bloody clothing was scattered about for hundreds of feet.

A bloody handkerchief was discovered on the ground beside her. Another bloody cloth had been stuffed into the crevice of a nearby tree. Beside the cemetery gate lay her gloves and a comb that had been in her hair. A ring and bracelet she had been wearing the night before were gone, as was her purse. Police believed Laura had been killed somewhere along the road and then her body dragged into the cemetery.

Vagrants in the area and anyone who aroused suspicion were quickly arrested and brought in for questioning. A New York native named Thomas Reilly was brought in due to scratches he bore on his face. Launey Williams was brought in as well, as he had a criminal past. John O'Brien, a New Hampshire native, was held by authorities after being randomly questioned and giving information about himself that proved to be false. One by one, men were arrested and subsequently let go when it was discovered there was nothing to tie them to the murder of Laura Regester.

The investigation then turned closer to home. Perhaps it was not a stranger who had killed the young woman. Laura's sister, Lillian, told police that Laura's life had been threatened many times by an elderly gentleman who was smitten with her. The latest threat had been just days before the murder, and Laura had remarked to Lillian, "I'll be lucky if I escape being killed before my marriage." Notices were broadcast across the eastern states to be on the lookout for this barber and musician named Clarence Chase. Laura enjoyed singing and had engaged in several musical performances with Clarence. However, her family said she became afraid of him when he tried to gain her romantic interest, and she eventually went out of her way to avoid him. Clarence was located in Massachusetts and provided a sound alibi concerning his whereabouts on the night of the murder.

Going on a tip they had received, police made plans to drag a pond near the murder scene for Laura's bracelet, ring and purse. A man, Charles Barr, who was discovered attempting to sell a bracelet in Los Angeles to obtain the money to attend a prizefight, was brought in for questioning when it was declared the bracelet matched the one the dead woman had been wearing. However, Barr was released when it was discovered that the jewelry was vastly different. Several times, police made statements to the press that they knew exactly who the killer was but were waiting for just the right moment to arrest him. But as alibis checked out and suspects were cleared, the trail began to run cold.

Suspicion fell on many people, including Laura's thirty-three-year-old fiancé, who lived with his father on Dudley Street. Police found it odd that he did not go to the Regester family home until about five hours after the body was discovered. He claimed that he had been at the A.A. Green Company on Point Street, where he was employed as a jeweler, when he received the news at about one o'clock that afternoon. They also found it strange that although Laura had told everyone her wedding was scheduled to take place on June 12, 1909, Charles insisted there had been no wedding date set. Also scrutinized was the ex-husband. Laura's family told police that she had divorced Ernest due to his ill treatment of her. Ernest's mother, however, said that it was Laura who had shown mistreatment and that her actions had broken her son's heart and mind, leaving him unbalanced. The young man had since been determined to be suffering from insanity on two different occasions and committed to the state mental hospital. Laura's friends reported to authorities that she had told them Ernest still visited her, although they had been divorced for four years, and that she had to keep explaining to him that she was engaged to be married to another man. Both men were eventually excluded as suspects.

Reward money for any information leading to the arrest of the killer soon totaled over $1,000 and included contributions from the mayor, as well as the D&W Fuse Company, where Laura had been employed. Yet such information never came. Police called the Regester murder one of the greatest mysteries in the annals of Rhode Island crime. Laura Regester lies in her grave at Locust Grove Cemetery on Elmwood Avenue in Providence.

GEORGE NELSON KENYON'S TUMULTUOUS AND TRAGIC LIFE

Wealthy Hotel Owner Kills His Carpenter

There was no one in Narragansett who was impartial when it came to George Nelson Kenyon, proprietor of the Ocean House hotel. You either loved him or hated him. George was born in Saybrook, Connecticut, on July 1, 1832, to Jane (Knowles) and James Kenyon, a sea captain. Following in his father's footsteps, he took his first sea voyage at the age of fifteen and would continue to occasionally ride the ocean until 1871.

In August 1857, George married Susan Catherine Saunders, and though the couple would never have any birth children, they adopted infant Herbert S. Greenwood in 1865. George had a great interest in real estate, and in 1870, he purchased the Ocean House on Caswell Street in Narragansett, which had been built the previous year for Mrs. S.L. Reed. The hotel became highly successful with the elite summer crowd, and George was known as an extremely attentive and accommodating host. But to the regular locals, he proved to be a thorn in many sides.

Obsessed with politics, George attended town meetings and angrily made his complaints clear. In 1882, he publicly accused the Town of Narragansett of mismanagement, unfair tax assessments, violation of oaths, illegal expenditures and dereliction in their duties. It was said his ire was lit when the town raised the value of his property from $10,000 to $12,000. George collected signatures of property owners to get a special meeting scheduled. Locals referred to the event as "Captain Kenyon's meeting," and he used the opportunity to convey long speeches about how unprofessionally the town was run. He felt that money for improvement was not divided equally between the north and south ends of town. In addition, bridges had been constructed over the river that ran between his properties, and he threatened to blow them up with dynamite if they were not removed. Many believed George was crazy.

He was definitely eccentric. One room of his house was filled with rare curiosities, and another held an array of firearms and other war-related items. He used profane language but didn't drink, preferring strong tea and tobacco to intoxicants. A shrewd businessman, he would get an elaborate plan in his head and push toward it, no matter how illogical. An idea to sail around the world led him to build his own yacht at a cost of $8,000. Those who saw it commented that it would be lucky to make it as far as Block Island. Two more yachts were constructed: *Redemption* and *Retribution*. He kept them not far from a little white cottage he built just above the bathing beach and named Mount Zion. He intended to sail the yachts to Mount Zion on Judgment Day.

In 1885, George purchased the snuff mill and birthplace of Gilbert Stuart in Saunderstown. He went into business there, selling ground flour and cornmeal. The following year, he was in Butler Asylum in Cranston. His periods of melancholy that followed each failed dream and his temper-fueled politics caused the state to admit him to the psychiatric hospital. However, he appealed the decision, and a hearing was held to determine if he was insane and dangerous. He was released after bringing forth ninety witnesses in his defense and then attempted to sue the six men who had been active in getting him committed, asking for $15,000 in damages for malicious prosecution.

Now a museum, the Gilbert Stuart House in Saunderstown witnessed the murder of a carpenter. *Vintage postcard from the collection of the author.*

The following year, George's wife left him and went to live with a dressmaker friend in Providence. She left instructions at the post office to hold her mail. When the postal clerk refused George's demand to give him her mail, George contacted the postmaster general and explosively relayed that the post office had "gone to the devil." A postal agent was immediately sent to the Ocean House to discuss the problem, and there he found George with two revolvers and an armed guard. When the agent told George he had no right to his wife's mail, he was thrown off the property. George then went to Providence and took all his wife's belongings. The next year, fueled with a new dream, he took out a patent on a dumping barge he invented for unloading coal and grain.

The Ocean House was bringing in over $5,000 per year, but George's estranged wife refused to run it with him any longer, so he put the hotel up for sale. His advertisement included the strange comment, "Its proprietor is one of the best known men in the United States. One who isn't weak-kneed or liable to grow weary and fall by the wayside."

George moved to the Gilbert Stuart property and hired the fifty-eight-year-old recently widowed John McGuinness to do renovations there. After toiling for two months and being paid only two dollars, John went to George to discuss the matter. There, on the property on January 14, 1890, George pointed a Winchester rifle at his employee's chest and fired a fatal shot. He

The Gilbert Stuart House and Museum, as it appears today, is a popular summer destination. *Photograph taken by the author.*

claimed it was in self-defense, but the trial, with his wife testifying for the prosecution, resulted in a fifteen-year prison term for manslaughter.

Three years later, George's wife passed away, and he appealed the will from prison, suing one of her family members to reclaim marital property. The court ruled that he did indeed have a legal right to his wife's property, but he would not live long enough to possess it. Kidney disease was taking a heavy toll on him, and he died at the Rhode Island State Prison hospital on August 25, 1900, at the age of sixty-eight, after serving just seven years of his sentence. He was laid to rest in Riverside Cemetery. The Ocean House hotel went out of business in 1917 and was torn down.

THE ALIBI OF ROBERT LATIMER

A Man Claims He Was Out of Town during His Mother's Murder

Robert Latimer was known and liked all over Westerly. The owner of Pawcatuck Woolen Mills, he resided with his wife, Mary; their son, Robert Irving; and their Irish housekeeper, Mary McGlynn. However, his likeability was not enough

The Potter Hill Mill is presently falling to ruin. *Photograph taken by the author.*

to save his career when his manufacturing business began to wane in 1887. Deciding a change was in order, Robert packed up and moved his family to Jackson, Michigan. For the younger Robert, the move meant leaving behind all he had come to know in his twenty-two years, including the friends he had made at Westerly High School and the people with whom he attended church.

Five years after the move, the elder Robert mysteriously died. While authorities believed the death was an intentional murder brought about by poisoning, they could find nothing to positively make such a determination. The fifty-seven-year-old man left an insurance policy worth $11,500. Of that amount, $8,000 would go to his wife, and $3,500 would go to his son. It was noted that, after his wife's demise, the remainder of her share would revert to their son.

The younger Robert had gone on to become a druggist and owned West End Pharmacy in Jackson. His father's death left him living alone with his forty-eight-year-old mother. On January 24, 1893, Robert left town aboard a train, heading for Detroit. He had told his clerk at the drugstore that a friend had passed away, and he was going to the funeral to serve as a pallbearer. That afternoon, he checked into a Detroit hotel.

Mary Latimer had hired a man named Harry Nicholls to come and wallpaper the house. When Nicholls arrived there at nine o'clock the

84

following morning, he rang the doorbell but got no response. After turning the knob and finding the door locked, he began ringing the doorbell again. The lady who lived next door happened to notice the man at the Latimers' door and went over to him, commenting that she had not seen Mary at all that morning. Together, they ventured around the house toward the cellar door. Nicholls pulled it open, and they were able to gain entrance to the house. The neighbor thought that perhaps Mary was sick, so she quietly made her way up the stairs and toward the bedroom while Nicholls waited. She slowly pushed the bedroom door open to find the bed empty. "Mary?" she called. "Mary?"

Suddenly, Nicholls heard an earth-shattering scream. He started running up the stairs as the neighbor woman shrieked, "She's killed! She's murdered!" There on the bedroom floor, Mary lay in a pool of blood. As word of the crime spread, friends knew it was critical to let Robert know what had happened to his mother, but no one had any idea how to reach him in Detroit. For the next few days, authorities reported that they had no clues in the murder. But on January 30, Robert was arrested.

The trial, which began on April 8 of that year, brought forth shocking and damning evidence against the twenty-eight-year-old. Employees of the railroad testified that he had gone to Detroit on the twenty-fourth but returned to Jackson later that night. After midnight, he once again climbed onto the train and went back to Detroit. The maid at the hotel where he was registered testified that he had not used the bed in his room on the night of the twenty-fourth.

Detroit barber William Henry Johnson provided even more evidence for the prosecution. He stated that on the afternoon of the twenty-fifth, Robert had come into his shop trembling and asked for a quick shave. He also asked if he could use the sink to wash up. Johnson happened to glance over at Robert while he was drying his hands and saw what resembled blood on the towel. He then noticed a bloodstained cuff on Robert's shirt. When he mentioned it, Robert explained that he had recently had a bloody nose. About to depart from the shop, Robert went to the door, nervously looked down the street in both directions and then passed out.

Throughout the trial, Robert gave off an air of cool confidence, smiling as if he didn't have a care in the world. But that all changed on May 6, when, after just seventeen minutes of deliberations, the jury returned with a verdict of guilty. Robert would be sentenced to life in prison for the first-degree murder of his mother.

By summer, prison guards had seen a major change in Robert. The egotism was gone, and he displayed what appeared to be symptoms of insanity. They never knew when he would eject loud cries, break out into song or begin talking to himself. They also observed him going into what appeared to be long trances. But the prisoner was apparently crazy like a fox. An investigation showed that Robert was involved in a plot to blow up the prison. Accomplices on the outside had been providing necessities, and a collection of explosives was discovered in the prison walls.

After a stint in solitary confinement, Robert worked to gain the trust of the guards. One of the prison employees, who often lunched with the prisoners, became particularly interested in spending private time with the young man. Robert had let the guard in on an alleged secret. His tale concerned an island not far from where he had once lived in Westerly. There on that island, according to Robert, was buried $2,800. The guard hoped to eventually be able to put together a map of the treasure site.

The prison druggist had provided Robert with prussic acid when he requested it for use in preparing photographic plates. One evening, Robert mixed the acid into two cups of hot chocolate and took them to the aforementioned guard, as well as another. Once the guards fell unconscious, Robert got the keys to the prison, grabbed a rifle and walked out the front door. Twenty miles from the prison, he entered a store in Jerome and attempted to buy a pair of shoes. Realizing that the clerk recognized him, he quickly fled and raced down the railroad tracks. A group of men from the store went in pursuit of him, and he was finally taken down and held there until police arrived. On his way back to the prison, he voluntarily told police that he had planned that escape for about a year. And upon learning that one of the guards had died from the ingestion of acid, he claimed that he was sorry and had intended only for them to fall asleep. He was placed back in solitary confinement and began to cry once the door was closed.

For years, people continued to talk about the grisly murder of Mary Latimer. It was believed that she had been shot once in her bed after retiring for the night and had managed to get up and make her way to the window before her head took a second bullet and she fell over backward. But there were some who believed that the real killer had not been caught and that Robert had been incarcerated due to purely circumstantial evidence. In December 1935, Robert Irving Latimer was pardoned for the crime and released from jail. He was seventy years old.

MURDER

THE KINGSTON TRAIN STATION MURDER
Three Men Are Found Dead in Old Railway Station

Railroad section foreman John Smith and track patrolman Fred Babcock were passing the old Kingston train depot at about four o'clock on the afternoon of January 30, 1916, when they saw tools scattered in the doorway. Two Swedes, thirty-seven-year-old Oscar Olsen and his brother, thirty-five-year-old Gustave Olsen, worked as section hands for the New York, New Haven & Hartford Railroad and were living there in the old depot about one mile from Kingston Station. Smith and Babcock weren't happy about such reckless care of the tools and began walking toward the entryway to summon the Olsens and instruct them to pick up the mess. As they entered the shack, they saw the Olsens lying motionless on the floor. Sheriff Wilcox and a physician were called for at once. The doctor determined that the cause of both deaths was murder and that it had occurred only a few hours earlier. In addition to the Swedes, another man lay dead in the room: forty-year-old William H. Rhodes, the son of Thomas Rhodes of Slocum. Of African American descent, he worked as a stonemason and was well known for conducting an illegal bootleg liquor business.

All three men had been shot at close range and then mutilated with an axe. It was believed, from the position of the bodies, that Rhodes had been shot twice in the head from behind while trying to make his way toward the door. One bullet had passed through his neck, severing the jugular vein, and another had gone through his ear and lodged in the cheekbone. His head was badly mangled, a contusion on the right side of the temple appearing to be the result of some blunt object he was struck with after he was already dead. One of his fingers also bore a gunshot wound, and a bloody axe lay on the ground beside his right hand. Oscar Olsen lay right beside him, a gunshot wound through his cheek and the bullet lodged in his nose. A second bullet had passed through his temple and a third through the back part of his skull. The back of his head was severely crushed on one side, and the gashes indicated that he had been struck with an axe two times, once with the blunt end and once with the blade.

To the right of Rhodes lay Gustave Olsen, who had been shot just below the center of his forehead, near his right eye, and had his face brutally crushed. The bodies were taken to the undertaking rooms of Joseph William Ineson in Wakefield while police conducted their investigation. The Olsens did not seem to have any criminal record, but Rhodes had a reputation as a pickpocket and had been arrested several times for illegal alcohol sales.

The Kingston Railroad Station was built in 1875. *Photograph courtesy of the Library of Congress.*

Inside the old depot, in the room where the bodies were discovered, police found three liquor bottles on the table. One had not yet been opened, and the others were partly emptied.

The last time anyone had seen the Olsens was the previous night, when they and Rhodes had gone to Edward Perry Tucker's store in West Kingston to buy groceries. Neighbors saw their lights go off that night at about ten o'clock but never heard the gunshots that followed. Police came up with the theory that the triple murder had been the result of a well-planned robbery in which the killer waited until a train was in the process of making its noisy passing before executing the shots. The Olsens had worked hard and saved a good sum of money, and many local people knew this. Rhodes had also accumulated quite a bit of cash and, the week before his murder, had shown several people a roll of more than $200. Detectives made the rounds of local saloons looking for suspects. It was learned that another member of the section gang had been staying with the Olsens. The search for him didn't go on for long, as James Rego Mellow soon surrendered himself to the Providence police. The thirty-three-year-old Portuguese man, who was the son of Joseph Mellow of Bristol, later testified at his trial, facing first-degree murder charges in Rhodes's death. For three hours, he gave the jury a very detailed account of his every move on the night of the murders.

Mellow stated that he had met Oscar Olsen in Milwaukee about ten years earlier. He and the Olsen brothers were traveling men, going where the work was, and they occasionally ran into one another over the years. He claimed that he had arrived in Kingston on the Wednesday before the murders to begin working for the Kingston railroad. On that fateful night, he had gone to the store with Oscar to get groceries, leaving Gus and Rhodes at the shack with another man whom he knew only as "Nick." Rhodes had brought whiskey and poured drinks for the men, but Mellow claimed he didn't partake of it. When they returned from the store, it was near dusk, and he and Oscar carried firewood into the shack while Rhodes, Nick and Gus went on to the store. When the men returned, they enjoyed more liquor provided by Rhodes, and the Olsens paid him for each drink. Gus opened a ham he had purchased but was too intoxicated to cook it, so Mellow got out a large frying pan and prepared the meat. Mellow said there were three chairs in the kitchen, and because all were taken up, Gus had to stand.

Once the ham was done, Rhodes immediately began to eat out of the pan, and Mellow told him not to do that. The shack contained three pans, one for each of the men who were staying there, as well as three individual coffee pots. Gus also began to put up a fuss about the pan, and Oscar suddenly hit him, knocking him down. Yelling at Gus to get up, Oscar kicked his brother hard, leaving a bruise. The jury listened to Mellow's version of what occurred that night as the drunken foray counted down to murder.

Mellow said he and Oscar returned to the store, and he waited outside while Oscar went in and purchased some fresh pork for forty-five cents. Rhodes soon made his way to the store, went inside and talked to Oscar, purchased some tobacco and left. When Oscar came out, the two men intended to return to the shack, but Oscar wanted to take a roundabout route, as he explained that he wanted to avoid Rhodes, who was trying to collect more money for the liquor he had served. The time was about 8:15 p.m. They returned to the shack, and Mellow cracked some eggs into the large frying pan and prepared another meal. He then decided that he was going to take the train for Westerly. He searched for his rubber boots, and when he was unable to find them, Gus said that Nick had taken them. The jury, as well as many other people, wondered if this person called "Nick" even existed. Mellow explained that he was a yellow-skinned man with a broad shape and had been wearing a red sweater that evening.

Mellow claimed he borrowed two dollars from Gus for his train ticket and left for the station. Once he arrived there, he asked someone when the train was due. He was told that it was due at 9:22 p.m. but was running late. Mellow thought he had time to use the bathroom, but when he came back out, the train was leaving. He ran to catch it but was not successful, so he sat there at the station until 11:00 p.m. and then decided to go back to the shack. He testified that the curtains were drawn, and there were no lights burning inside. He went to the door and knocked after he found it locked but wasn't let in, so he went up the stairs to the top part of the shack. He soon heard a strange noise and then a door slam shut. Descending the stairs, he went around to the back part of the structure and could now see a light through the curtain. He opened the back door and went inside. Oscar was sitting in one of the chairs sobbing heavily. Rhodes had returned and was standing at the table. Mellow said he saw Rhodes put a watch and a small purse of money in his pocket. He then pulled a revolver from his pocket and laid it on the table. It was at that point, he said, when he noticed Gus's body lying on the floor. "What's going on here?" he asked, horrified. Rhodes then allegedly pointed the revolver at him.

Mellow said he grabbed the frying pan off the stove and struck Rhodes with it, causing the gun to fall onto the table. Mellow struck him a second time, and the handle broke off the pan. Rhodes staggered, grabbing Mellow by the sweater and pulling off a button. Dazed and bleeding from the mouth, he held on to Mellow for support before shoving him backward. Mellow fell against Oscar, knocking the Swede out of the chair and onto the floor. There was blood on Oscar, and it stained Mellow's clothing. Rhodes then threw Mellow against a wall, he testified, and when he grabbed for the revolver, Rhodes struck him. The gun fell to the floor, and the two men both struggled to grab it. After knocking Rhodes down, Mellow got ahold of the gun. Rhodes grabbed the axe and came toward him, swinging the axe back with such force that it struck the wall.

At this point, Mellow told the court, he began to wonder if the gun even contained any bullets. "Will you give up?" he asked Rhodes. Without an answer, Rhodes made another swing with the axe, and the two men fell onto each other and landed on the floor. Mellow said he feared for his life and pulled the trigger. The bullet struck Rhodes in the neck; however, he raised his arm to take another swing with the axe. Mellow shot him a second time, and Rhodes fell flat on his back with the axe landing on the floor beside him. Mellow claimed he unlocked the front door and went outside, calling for help. He then went back in and saw that Rhodes's sweater was on fire from the gunshot. He rolled him over so that he could extinguish the fire and burned his fingers in the process. He then went over to Oscar, who was still alive. He picked him up off the floor and tried to get him to talk, but the Swede's life ebbed away right before his eyes.

Mellow stated that he went back outside and heard someone out there. "Who comes there?" he called. He told the jury it was "Nick" and that he warned him not to go into the shack because there had been trouble going on. He said that he became very scared at that moment that he was going to be blamed for the killings. He took off down the street, leaving Nick there. A short time later, however, he returned, and Nick was gone. He went back into the shack and took the money that was on the table, as well as two bottles of whiskey. After hiding himself in a coal car, he rode the train toward Providence. He still had the gun in his possession—a white-handled revolver that had once been crudely repaired. There were four cartridges in the gun and a vacant chamber, he said. As the train passed through East Greenwich, he tossed it from the coal car, along with his bloodstained coat. He wandered around Providence for several days before deciding to turn himself in to police. He testified that he knew people were going to be blaming him for killing the Olsens and that he wanted the truth known.

Numerous people testified on Mellow's behalf, most of them people who had employed him. The consensus was that he was an honest, hardworking man who had never given anyone cause for concern. However, his criminal record did not reflect that of a law-abiding citizen. At the age of eleven, he had been sent to reform school. He was sentenced for larceny in 1902 after stealing money from his mother's bureau, served three months in prison in 1909 for assault and was sentenced again in 1910 for reveling. The prosecution believed that Mellow had shot all three men and then attacked them with the axe when the bullets didn't kill them fast enough. It was thought that robbery was the motive, as the Olsens' pockets were turned inside out and ripped open, and Mellow had placed the watch in Rhodes's pocket to make him appear to be the thief.

The case of the *State of Rhode Island v. James Rego Mellow* was heard before the Washington County Superior Court in Kingston. Mellow was defended by a young lawyer named Clarence Emerson Roche, of Westerly, who had never tried a criminal case before. Roche had requested that the three bodies be removed from the vault in Wakefield, where they were being held, so that the defense could have them examined, but the request was denied. Allegedly, the bodies had been mutilated during the autopsies. Mellow was found guilty as charged for the first-degree murder of Rhodes and sent to the state prison in Cranston. By 1940, he had been transferred to the State Hospital for Mental Diseases.

THE CHRISTMAS EVE MURDER OF THOMAS MAIN
Elderly Man Is Killed in His Own Home

Christmas morning of 1915 found thirty-one-year-old Halsey Clarke Kenyon going about the business of running his farm. It was about 10:00 a.m. when he jumped into his wagon, joined by one of his helpers, a Mr. Fiddes, to go pick up a load of sawdust. They had traveled about a mile, reaching the halfway point between Hopkinton City and Hope Valley, when Halsey's gaze was pulled toward a large, smoldering pile of ruins. Just the day before, it had been the site of Thomas Dorr Main's home. The seventy-year-old Thomas was a widower who lived alone, and Halsey had just visited with him three days earlier.

While the children of Hopkinton waited for Santa, Thomas Main was being murdered in his own home. *Vintage photograph courtesy of Hope Greene Andrews.*

MURDER

Halsey traveled on to his father's house, and sixty-year-old Charles Kenyon accompanied his son back to the Main property to investigate after enlisting the help of several other men. Charles had known Thomas for over fifty years and also had seen him just days earlier. Once they reached the site of the ruins, the men got out of the wagon and began to look through the wreckage. "I smell meat burning," Charles said. Not long after, one of the men called everyone's attention to his discovery. In the basement area, a partially cremated human body lay inside a wash boiler cover.

Medical examiner Asa Briggs was summoned and directed that the men pick up what bones remained. They did so, placing them in an old iron kettle found within the ruins. Thomas's watch was found near the body, and identification of the bones was not difficult. Thomas had had a very noticeable hump in his back, and the men present at the scene could clearly see a prominent crook in the spine lying before them.

Washington County sheriff John Wilcox and Deputy Charles Bennett later arrived at the conclusion that Main had been murdered when they were unable to locate his gun among the smoldering wreckage. However, an investigation carried out by police, the medical examiner and the coroner shed no light on what had happened. The *Hope Valley Advertiser* ran an announcement that read, "A reward of $500 will be paid for the detention, apprehension and conviction of any person or persons guilty of the murder of Thomas Main, by order of the Town Council of Hopkinton." The sheriff and deputy didn't let the case go cold. After several months of searching for clues, they were led to a thirty-three-year-old local well-digger named Welcome Andrew Main and a forty-four-year-old mill operative named John Barker. Both men were subsequently arrested in Hope Valley on an early Tuesday morning the following September, charged with murder and transported to the Westerly Police Station for questioning. At the station, the two men were placed in separate rooms. Welcome assured the police that he had nothing to do with any murder and that he had alibis for every moment during the day of December 24, 1915. Yet when asked about his movements that night, he had no answers to give.

John Barker quickly caved in to the questioning by Wilcox, Bennett and the captain of inspectors of the Providence Police Department, George Monahan. He offered a full confession. "I'll tell you all I know about this affair," he said.

Welcome Main planned to rob Thomas Dorr Main about three weeks before the night of the murder. I came out of the mill where I worked and

93

met Welcome Main and we started off together. We had Tom Barber's gun with us, for I stepped into the store and borrowed it as we went along the road. We then went out to Thomas's place and made a call. We knocked at the door and Thomas let us in. We had supper and stayed in the house until it was quite late. After a while, we came out and stood by a shed. Thomas was sitting in a lighted room. Welcome fired a couple of shots through the window at Thomas but did not hit him. Then Thomas came to the door with a lamp in one hand and a gun in the other. He opened the door and shouted, "For God's sake, what's the matter?"

John stated that Welcome then fired the revolver again. "Thomas fell backward into the house, the lighted lantern setting the house on fire," he said.

Welcome ran into the house and I laid down on the ground near the shed. Then Welcome took Thomas's gun and the money. He came back with the gun and Welcome gave me eight dollars which he said was my share of the money he took from Thomas, and that's all I got. And we went off and left the house to burn. We went up Thomas's house Saturday night before to do the job. We made out that we were drunk, but for some cause or other that I don't know, the job was not done. Welcome didn't tell me how much money he took from Thomas.

John told police that he believed Welcome was a distant relative of Thomas and that they seemed to be on friendly terms. Indeed, the elderly man was the cousin of Welcome's grandfather. Sandy-haired with hazel eyes, Welcome originally hailed from North Stonington and was the son of farmer Andrew Main and his wife, Loansa (Foster). At the time of his arrest, he and his wife, Pearl, had been married for six years.

"I did not receive but very little of the money and was warned to keep my mouth shut under penalty of death," John informed police.

Three days later, the two men were arraigned on a charge of murder, and both pleaded not guilty. They were held for the grand jury without bail. Welcome retained attorney Samuel King to represent him, while John hired John Dunn as his lawyer. Later, during testimony, Halsey Kenyon stated that, on the Sunday before the fire, Thomas had reported to him that Welcome and John had been at his home the night before until after midnight and that he had ordered them from the house as he did not want to burn up his wood for their accommodation. Charles Kenyon testified that the last time he had seen Thomas, the ill-fated man had mentioned that he had about $100 in his pocket.

Welcome and John were eventually both sentenced to the Rhode Island State Prison in Cranston, where Welcome was put to work in the prison's carpentry shop. Thomas Main had celebrated his seventieth birthday just four days before he was murdered. He was the second of two children born to Amos Main and Mary (Burton). His older brother had passed away in 1863 at the age of nineteen.

That Christmas Eve of 1915, as residents reveled in the peace and joy of the holiday, many stared out at the night sky above Hope Valley, strangely lit up above a secluded spot not far from Hopkinton City. Within the cause of that illumination, an innocent man suffered a horrendous death at the hands of two men he trusted.

MAN KNOWN AS THE HUMAN MONSTER ROAMS TOWN

A Well-Known Killer Is Discovered on Rural Streets

Isaac Goldstein couldn't get to the police fast enough. He had been peddling fruit that afternoon when suddenly he came face to face with a man being chased around the entire state. Goldstein's report was dated October 10, 1912. "I was on the road between Wyoming and Carolina when a man came out of the woods behind me and called me," he told police. He explained how he turned around to see the man standing in the road near a place where he had formerly worked. Goldstein recognized him and said his name. "He said, 'Hello, Goldstein. Give me some bananas?' I told him to take anything he wanted but not to touch me," he went on. "I also told him that I knew what kind of man he was and asked him what he was doing."

The man told Goldstein that he was just out for a little walk. Then he took the bananas and went into the woods. As soon as he was out of sight, Goldstein quickly galloped his horse toward the police station. He described the man as well dressed and in a good mood: "He smiled as he took the bananas and flung them back over his shoulder."

Police throughout the state were becoming extremely agitated by the cunning man with whom Goldstein had crossed paths. An escapee from the state prison, his capture was proving to be a game of cat and mouse. His

A killer at large was discovered not far from Wyoming, where the stables for Dawley's Tavern can be seen to the far left. *Vintage photograph courtesy of Hope Greene Andrews.*

name was Ernest Wilhelm Lorenz, and he had become known as the "insane murderer" and the "human monster" of Rhode Island. Two years earlier, he had been arrested for killing Gilbert Mann of Johnston. Mann had worked as a coachman and was transporting a passenger, sixty-one-year-old George Williams, along Hartford Pike on January 8, 1910, at about 4:00 p.m. when Lorenz suddenly appeared in the road and grabbed the horse's bridle.

"Hands up!" he ordered, pointing a revolver at the men. Williams did as he was told, but Mann grabbed the whip and tried to get the horse into action. "Stop or I'll shoot!" Lorenz warned.

Mann struck the horse again, and two gunshots rang out. As Mann slumped in his seat, Lorenz led the carriage over to the side of the road and ordered Williams to get out. He searched through Williams's pockets and became angry at finding only two cents. He then dragged Mann from the carriage by his collar and propped him up against a carriage wheel. Mann clung to the wheel desperately while Lorenz went through his pockets. He retrieved thirty-five cents and a gold watch before placing the dying man back in his seat. He then told Williams to get back in as well. "Do as I tell you! Stay there for ten minutes before you dare to go out onto the road or I will shoot you," Lorenz threatened Williams. He then hurried away from the scene. As soon as the thief was out of sight, Williams raced to a physician's office, and police were notified. Mann had been hit twice in the left side of his chest and succumbed to his injuries eight days later.

Williams described the highway bandit as being of German descent, about forty years old and neatly dressed right down to his bowtie. Police had received a similar description after a highway robbery the previous month. On December 24, 1909, fruit grower Harry Bartlett and his wife were driving along the same street when a man suddenly appeared in the road and shouted, "Hands up!" He then grabbed the reins and ordered Bartlett out of the buggy. With his finger on the trigger of his revolver, he searched Bartlett for weapons before rummaging around in his pockets. Mrs. Bartlett began to scream. Lorenz turned the gun on her and threatened, "I will blow your head off!"

He relieved his victim of a gold watch, a roll of bills and a penny, which he found in a vest pocket. "You are about as mean a sort of degenerate as might be found," Bartlett told him.

"Shut up!" Lorenz commanded.

On January 17, he struck again. Sanford Burton Jr. of North Providence was robbed on Lexington Road while on his way to work, having his gold watch and money taken by a German holdup man. The following day, Burton saw Lorenz on the street and quickly approached a nearby police officer to point him out. Lorenz was arrested and searched. He was found to be in possession of a revolver and a gold watch that had been stolen from William Comstock of Cranston during a holdup the previous week.

Lorenz told police his name was William Luder. It wasn't until later in the day that he admitted his true identity, adding that he was born in Germany on April 9, 1881; had arrived in America on October 14, 1903; rented a room on North Main Street; and was employed as a fancy cake baker. He fully admitted to robbing Burton and committing a staggering number of additional criminal acts that had taken place in Barrington, Warwick, Cranston, Johnston and North Providence. With one murder charge and fifteen charges of holdups and robberies, he was held without bail.

Lorenz continued to talk. He admitted that he regularly roamed the streets looking for women to assault and that he kept a notebook detailing each attack. Once the crime was publicized and the victim identified, he would add her name to his notes. It was always women he was seeking, he said, but when none was around, he would rob men.

Police began to wonder if Lorenz had been involved in the unsolved murder of Laura Regester in May 1910. The young woman's body was found at the Jewish Cemetery in Providence, and the killer was never discovered. Lorenz had come to America with a friend, who had secured a job at a sausage manufactory. The friend now told authorities that one day while driving past the Jewish Cemetery, Lorenz had said, "That's where the Regester girl was murdered." Lorenz relayed his in-depth knowledge of the crime to his friend and gave his thoughts on how he believed the killer had accomplished his task. To police, however, Lorenz denied any involvement in Regester's death.

Determined to be insane, he was placed in the prison psychiatric ward. Employed in the bakery there with two other men, he would rise early to begin his shift. On October 5, 1912, the guard on duty saw him in the bakery at 4:55 a.m. Five minutes later, he was gone. Having slipped quietly out into the yard, he stuck a garden hoe into the barred enclosure where a ladder was hanging on the wall and knocked it off the pegs. He then tied a cord around it and pulled it through the bars. The outside guards did not go on duty until 6:30 a.m.

Lorenz propped the ladder against the wall that surrounded the prison and climbed to his freedom. Police sent out a photo and description of the escapee: five feet, five inches in height, 152 pounds, short and stocky, chestnut brown hair and brown eyes. Wearing his prison uniform of gray trousers and a white cotton shirt, he was soon spotted in several different places. One witness saw him near a barn in Cranston. Another observed him riding a bike in Warwick. A man living near the prison was soon to report his bike missing from his property. Police in every Rhode Island town began searching for Lorenz and amped up the search after Goldstein's sighting. Three heavily armed guards raced to the stretch of land between Carolina and Wyoming, where they formed a posse to help comb the woods and marshes. Carrying revolvers and rifles, they searched for banana peels. Two days later, a local newspaper received a letter that was signed, "A Very Dear Friend of Lorenz." The letter read, "The cops of Providence are pretty slow when Lorenz can pass by College and Benefit Streets at 9:30 last night."

State residents were unable to sleep comfortably knowing that a man who had been diagnosed as having such afflictions as paranoid dementia, sexual perversion and insanity was out roaming the streets—a murderer and rapist, robber and sociopath. There's no telling how long it took for that fear to subside. Lorenz was never found.

MURDER

THE MYSTERIOUS DEATH OF
SENATOR CHARLES BURDICK
Politician Slain in His Home Remains a Mystery

Gertrude Burdick and her daughter, a local schoolteacher, had just returned home from a two-hour shopping trip in Westerly at 6:00 p.m. on the crisp autumn evening of October 17, 1930. Their comfortable home in Wood River Junction was the result of her husband's many years of hard work. Charles Burdick was a prosperous farmer and wood dealer and had also served as a Rhode Island state senator. He was well liked and highly respected by all who knew him. Gertrude's daughter let her out of the car before she drove into the garage. Gertrude made her way up to the side veranda and there saw a sight that stunned her.

Charles Burdick lay on the floor, his body seemingly lifeless. Gertrude believed that her husband must have suffered some type of shock and screamed for her daughter to get help. She then rushed into the house and returned with a glass of water to try and revive Burdick. Her daughter ran to the nearby home of Charles Plympton, to whom her sister was married. Soon, she returned with Plympton, and he examined Burdick's body, only to realize that the man had expired. The three of them then went into the house, where a horrific scene awaited. Evidence of massive violence was

The railroad tracks through Wood River Junction, not far from the secluded home of Charles Burdick. *Vintage photograph courtesy of Hope Greene Andrews.*

99

strewn everywhere in the aftermath of some terrible struggle. A bullet was discovered lying on the floor, and there was a hole in the windowpane through which the bullet had entered. Plympton went to look over Burdick's body again and determined that he had been shot. Westerly medical examiner Michael Scanlon was immediately contacted, and he, in turn, contacted the Rhode Island State Police at the Hope Valley barracks. Soon, Scanlon and a trooper arrived at the Burdick house. Scanlon examined the body while the trooper investigated the scene, and it was learned that nine bullets had been fired at the victim from a .38-caliber revolver and that he had put up a fierce struggle. Several of the shots were fired at him at very close range, including one behind and one in front of the left ear and three in the stomach. The shot police believed to be fatal was under the left eye.

After police had reconstructed the scene, they felt that whoever had killed the former senator had patiently waited for his wife and daughter to leave and then looked through the window to see Burdick sitting on a backless chair in the kitchen, where he was repairing a cream separator. They believed the killer shot at him through the window, the bullet penetrating his back. They felt Burdick then rose and started toward the window while two more bullets were fired at him, breaking his right wrist. At that time, Burdick was believed to have removed his coat, and he threw it into a corner before the shooter came into the house and a struggle ensued. That whole area of the house was spattered with blood, and the trail led out to the veranda, where it was assumed Burdick finally passed out and died.

The pockets on Burdick's clothing were turned inside out and were empty, leading police to conclude that robbery was the motive for the murder. It was well known that Charles regularly carried large sums of money with him. Gertrude checked the money they usually kept in the house, which amounted to several thousand dollars, and found none of that to be missing. The sixty-seven-year-old wood dealer and former politician, and the son of Charles Burdick and Sarah (Tanner), had spent his whole life in Charlestown and had no enemies that anyone knew of. He had lived a quiet, peaceful life with his wife, Gertrude (Hoxsie), whom he had married in Hopkinton on January 17, 1891, and their two daughters, Sarah and Ethel.

No one came forward to report hearing any gunshots that day, as the house sat in a lonely, isolated section of the village. The Rhode Island State Police brought in several men they thought might be potential suspects but turned all of them loose when their alibis checked out. Nearly a dozen men were brought in for questioning, and although all were released, they were told not to leave Charlestown, as footprints near the Burdick home were found to be identical to those of one of the men. Even Charles Plympton was questioned, leaving police confident that he had nothing to do with the murder. Police informed the public that an item found at the scene would be instrumental in identifying the killer. Though they would not say what the item was, rumors swirled that it was part of a broken tooth or a set of false teeth belonging to the killer and lost during the struggle. Others claimed they'd heard it was a set of keys.

Scanlon had the body removed to Westerly, where it would undergo a series of X-rays to determine the location of the bullets that remained in his body. Burdick was then transported to Avery Funeral Home in Hope Valley, where the funeral was held at two o'clock in the afternoon on October 21. He was later laid to rest in the Burdick family plot in Charlestown. The police, feeling confident that robbery was the motive and that the crime had been carefully planned out, collected every clue they could possibly find. Two days before the funeral, they arranged for a pumping truck from the Charlestown-Richmond Fire Department to come and pump out the well on the property, hoping to locate a murder weapon. Each hope they had of cracking the case fell apart, one after another.

Few people passed by the Burdick home, as it was far from the main road. Whoever had killed Burdick knew the immediate movements of his family, as his daughter usually took her mother shopping in Westerly on Saturdays but had decided to go on Friday of that week instead. The killer must have known that plans had changed for that day and that Burdick would be home alone. Still, no evidence leading police to the killer ever turned up, and they finally declared that the murder would go down in the annals of unsolved crimes. They were right.

MARY GARDINER IS DEALT EVERY BAD CARD IN THE DECK
A Husband Disappears and a Granddaughter Is Murdered

Charles S. Gardiner kissed his wife and two children goodbye. A machinist by trade, he had decided to go scout around Providence for employment there. Telling his family he'd be back on Saturday, he left his home near Bank Street in Hope Valley and took off on his journey. The year was 1881, and Mary Jane Gardiner; her fourteen-year-old daughter, Lillian; and her thirteen-year-old son, George, would never see Charles again.

Like Charles Gardiner, many local residents obtained jobs in area mills, such as these employees of the Mystic Mill in Hope Valley. *Vintage photograph from the collection of the author.*

Charles had married Mary Jane Protesta, an Italian immigrant, on November 5, 1865, in Taunton, Massachusetts, when she was just nineteen years old and he was twenty-four. The son of Sylvester and Mary Elizabeth Gardiner, he had grown up in Richmond and later relocated to Hope Valley, where he worked as a jeweler and toiled in local mills. Mary worked in the mills as well, employed as a spooler tender.

When Charles failed to return from his trip to the city, his sister, Mrs. Horace Slocum, was certain he had become the victim of foul play. Most family members agreed with her. Mary didn't want to give up hope, but finally, after several years, she applied for his pension, as he had served in the Civil War with Company C of the Third Rhode Island Artillery. Her application was denied, however, as she could not furnish proof that her husband was dead.

Nineteen years after her husband's disappearance, Mary relocated to Abbington, Massachusetts, to live with her daughter, Lillian, the wife of Fred G. Ashley, and their small daughter, Edith Mildred. She applied to the State of Massachusetts for the pension, and it was granted to her. Still, the mystery of what had happened to Charles hung over the Gardiner family and all of Hope Valley.

MURDER

In April 1906, the pension office contacted Mary and informed her that Charles's pension never should have been allotted to her as Charles had been alive until just recently. A Fitchburg woman had contacted authorities in Massachusetts seeking state aid and informed them that her husband died of heart disease on February 22 at their home on Boutelle Street. The woman identified him as none other than Charles S. Gardiner. Mary thought there must surely be some mistake. But there was no mistake. The woman had met Charles the year after he left home. The following year, they were wed, despite the fact that she was twenty-two and he was a forty-two-year-old married man. Charles had obtained work as a clock repairman and told her that he was widowed and had no children. Together, they welcomed four offspring in the years that followed.

The woman in Fitchburg was in disbelief over the entire matter, stating that Charles was held in very high esteem in town, known for being very industrious and providing for his family wonderfully. When the court declared that Mary was Charles's legal wife, the other woman was wrought with embarrassment. Not only was she truly an unmarried woman, but she also had four children out of wedlock with no legal claim to their own father. Mary was devastated as well, realizing that the husband she had been mourning had actually abandoned her and her children. But her fate would not soon improve.

Mary's granddaughter Edith, now seventeen and a recent graduate of Abbington High School, had been dating twenty-one-year-old Samuel Turner Stetson Jr. of Rockland, who had recently given up his job as an edge trimmer in a shoe factory. He had been showering Edith with attention for months, and finally they became engaged. On December 28, he paid a visit to her house on Thaxter Avenue after she had returned his gifts and told him she did not want to see him anymore. Her mother, Lillian, was home at the time but had some things to pick up at the store, so she left. A short time later, Samuel and Edith left the house, too, walking down the road toward town. As they neared the Dunbar Street School, they walked into the schoolyard and sat on the steps at the rear of the building.

Lillian was approaching the school as she made her way back home from the store when she heard gunshots and a girl's scream. She immediately recognized the voice and began running toward the back of the school. In just moments, Edith staggered into her arms. "I have been shot!" she cried. "I told him he must give me up, and Sam shot me! He told me he was sorry!"

Samuel lay on the bottom step with the revolver on the step just above him. After shooting Edith, he had dropped to his knees, prayed and then dispensed a bullet into his chest. Hanging on to the last threads of life, he would be dead within an hour.

Edith was taken to Brockton Hospital, where the bullet in her own chest was removed. Prospects for her recovery were good, but the following afternoon, she began to fail rapidly and died at 3:00 p.m. For Mary Gardiner, strength wasn't a virtue that was needed at random moments. It was a way of life for one who seemed to have been dealt every bad card in the deck.

LOVE, ADULTERY AND THE MURDER OF FREDERICK BISHOP

A Woman Sees Herself as the Victim When Her Lover Kills Her Husband

Frederick Howard Bishop and Peleg Everett Champlin were co-workers at the Rhode Island Company, which owned the largest system of electric trolleys in the state. Frederick was a motorman, and Peleg was an inspector. The two of them got along flawlessly, and for a while, Peleg even boarded at the Bishop home. Unfortunately, the men had more in common than they thought—specifically, Frederick's wife, Leah.

The son of Gilbert Bishop and Mary Knight, Frederick had first married Sarah Booth in 1891, when he was twenty-one years old. She passed away just eight years later. Frederick then married Leah C. Generoux, nine years his junior. Shortly after their marriage, Fred and Leah both secured jobs at the Sockanosset School for Boys in Cranston and lived there at the school, where Leah was a cook and Fred was a steward. By 1915, the couple was running a boardinghouse out of their Providence home, lodging a teacher, a chemist, a factory salesman and a laundress.

Peleg, a native of Charlestown, was born in 1872 to Nathan Champlin and Mary Tucker. In 1894, he had married Hannah Burdick. She died in 1912, and the following year, Peleg took a fancy to his co-worker's wife.

On the night of November 23, 1915, Leah returned to her home on Westminster Street in Providence, after spending two days with relatives in Pawtucket, to find her husband dead on the floor of the sitting room, his head crushed and bearing three bullet holes. During their investigation, police surmised that a struggle had begun in Frederick's bedroom and ended in the sitting room. They detained and questioned two of the boarders as possible suspects: Thomas MacArthur, whose bedroom adjoined the sitting room,

Trolleys, like those Frederick Bishop and Peleg Champlin worked on, were a popular mode of transportation. *Photograph courtesy of the Library of Congress.*

and J.A. Launey, whose bedroom was right beside Frederick's. Both suspects stated that they had arrived home at about two o'clock that morning and had heard no disturbance. On the floor of the sitting room, police discovered a leather revolver holster and a constable's badge. These were shown to Leah, who reported that they were not the property of her husband.

Later that night, Peleg presented himself at the police station to make a written confession. He stated that Frederick had asked him to come over after they both finished up work early that morning. Once at the house, Frederick asked Peleg if he had been with Leah. When Peleg said no, Frederick allegedly attacked him. Peleg stated that a struggle ensued and that he hit Frederick over the head with a blackjack in self-defense and then shot him in the head three times with a revolver. Peleg was arrested and held without bail.

When police questioned Leah, she made no attempt to hide the fact of her adulterous relationship with Peleg. She admitted that the affair had begun when he was boarding at their house. "I was surprised, but

I reciprocated his affection," she said. Explaining that she always called Peleg by his middle name, Everett, she said, "I loved Everett Champlin, and he had loved me for nearly two years. I told my husband of my love for Everett, but Frederick refused to give me up. He said he would take me away but that he did not have the money to go anywhere, and I pleaded with my husband that, in another part of the world, I could forget about Everett and be true."

Leah expressed shock at the turn of events, explaining that she had never heard the two men quarrel or make threats to each other regarding her involvement with both of them. "No one could have been more surprised or pained than I was when I learned of the awful tragedy which had occurred as the result of our love," she said. "Had Frederick taken me away, I am sure that nothing like this would have happened. But it is too late."

Leah appeared to believe that she was an innocent victim in the matter and felt she had done nothing wrong. "I still had such a high degree of respect for my husband that I would not leave him and tried to be true to him, although I loved another," she said. "If Everett had loved me as much as he said so many times, he would never have brought this sorrow upon me. It cannot be true love when a man will do such a terrible thing, even for love."

Peleg pleaded not guilty to the charge of murder and was defended in court by attorney Walter Barney. On December 22, 1915, with the consent of the attorney general, he pleaded nolo to a lesser charge of second-degree murder and was sentenced to serve twenty-seven years at the Rhode Island State Prison in the Howard complex in Providence. However, Peleg did not live long enough to serve his full sentence. Ironically, he died the same way as his co-worker had. On April 19, 1930, two gunmen arrived at the prison with the intention of breaking two convicted armed robbers out of the jail. When Peleg saw the men press a revolver into the side of the guard at 2:20 p.m., he pushed the alarm button. One of the gunmen, Walter Sullivan, shot and killed him. He was laid to rest beside his wife.

Frederick had been buried fifteen years earlier, and his grave was marked with a stone that included both his and Leah's names. On it, her birthdate is carved. Yet she apparently does not lie beside him in death.

RUTH PECKHAM'S LOW TOLERANCE FOR HER HUSBAND'S WANDERING EYE

Woman Kills Husband Who Shows Attention to Others

Ruth Peckham didn't like her husband flirting with other women. In fact, to do so might have had fatal consequences. On the Tuesday evening of September 6, 1932, thirty-five-year-old Ruth and her forty-three-year-old spouse, Albert, decided to attend a dance in Kingston. Late that night, they returned to their home, which had formerly served as the Woodville Schoolhouse on Woodville Road. Ruth was in a foul mood. As far as she was concerned, Albert had paid far too much attention to the other women at the dance, and that wasn't something she took lightly. As he went into the bedroom and began undressing for a restful slumber, Ruth went and got their .32-caliber revolver and fired four shots at him.

Half clad, Albert ran for his life. With a bullet wound on the right side of his face, another on his right arm and two more to his right shoulder and right hip, he was bleeding profusely as he raced an eighth of a mile toward the home of forty-three-year-old shoe store clerk Thomas Fidler and his roommate, Edward Boucher. Arriving at their door, he pounded hard and

Although the sermons at the Woodville church taught residents that killing was wrong, Ruth Peckham was determined to put a stop to her husband's flirting. *Vintage photograph courtesy of KarenLu LaPolice.*

cried out, "My wife has shot me three or four times! She might be right here and shoot me again!"

Thomas and Edward opened the door and let him in. Albert began to light a lamp, but the two men quickly pushed his hand away from it, explaining that Ruth might have followed him and that if she saw the light in the window, she might fire the weapon into the house. The men knew they had to get Albert to a doctor quickly. In addition to the bullet wounds, his jaw felt as if it might have been fractured. One of the bullets had even knocked out several teeth. Thomas carefully exited the house and made his way through the dark toward his automobile. He started it up and helped Albert get into the passenger's side. Without illuminating anything on the vehicle, they made their way toward the home of Dr. James O'Hear in Hope Valley.

Ruth had indeed followed her husband but arrived too late to inflict any further damage. Edward quietly knelt down by an upstairs bedroom window as she began pounding on the door. "Is my husband in there?" she called out. Edward raised himself up enough to look out the window. He saw Ruth standing at the door with a flashlight in her hand. In the other hand, she gripped the revolver. "He has made very insulting remarks to me tonight!" she angrily explained. "He was flirting with other women at the dance and paying attention to them!" Edward remained in his hiding spot. "I hope he dies!" Ruth continued on.

Albert was not going to die, however. Dr. O'Hear told Thomas to take Albert to the South County Hospital in Wakefield. The physician then contacted the Hope Valley State Police barracks and notified authorities of the crime that had taken place earlier that evening. Corporal Harvey and Trooper Raymond Blake hurried toward the Peckham residence, which was now ablaze with fire. Inside, a large, charred mass lay atop a cot. The men assumed it was Ruth, but due to the smoke and flames, they could not get close enough to make any positive determination.

By 7:42 a.m., the house had been reduced to smoking ruins. Investigators were able to go in and determine that Ruth's body was not inside. A search of the area began, with Trooper Blake and twenty-four-year-old Woodville resident and railroad laborer Floyd Church noticing footprints on a dirt road that led toward the woods. Just as they were about to enter the treed area, two bullets whizzed past them. The men ducked. "Go back!" Trooper Blake told Floyd. The policeman then went into the woods alone, scanning the area with his eyes. Suddenly, he saw Ruth standing beneath the trees about twenty-five feet from the edge of Woodville Road. Immediately, she fired another bullet toward him. Trooper Blake ran toward Ruth, and as he grabbed for her, she stumbled, dropped the gun and fell to the ground. Soon, she was restrained, handcuffed and taken to the police barracks.

During questioning, Ruth was very defiant, having no remorse for her actions, to which she willingly admitted. There were still several bullets in the gun and many more stashed inside her pocket. She confessed to returning home at about three o'clock in the morning, after visiting Thomas and Edward's house, and setting her own house afire. She even confessed to shooting at her husband for the specific intent of killing him. Ruth Peckham had done nothing she regretted, aside from getting caught.

WILLIAM BROWN KILLS CHILD FOR SAYING ALPHABET INCORRECTLY

A Little Girl Who Can't Say the Letter P Is Brutalized

William Coggeshall Brown of South Kingstown had been married for just ten months. He and his new wife, Sarah Ann (Kenyon), would later become the parents of twelve children. However, why any woman would stay married and begin a family with a child killer is anyone's guess. Brown was born in Newport on April 11, 1792, to Peleg Brown and Mary Cornell (Coggeshall). A farmer, he was home on the evening of December 27, 1813, with his wife and their guests, Mr. and Mrs. Baker, when he decided it was time to practice the alphabet with a five-year-old girl who was residing with them. Little Mary Holloway recited the alphabet as she was told yet had some trouble when she got to the letter *p*. Brown ordered her to pronounce the letter correctly, but when she did not, it would prove a fatal mistake.

After painfully biting her ear, Brown angrily left the house and returned with several sticks he had gone to cut to use as whips. With barbaric force, he beat her mercilessly. Still, Brown did not feel this had been enough of a punishment for the child's failure to say the entire alphabet as he wanted it said. He picked up her small body and held it over the burning fire, eventually burning her to death. Without a word, his wife and houseguests stood and watched.

During a trial at the Washington County courthouse, Brown was represented by lawyers John Whipple and Levi Trotten. Forty-nine people testified before the trial was brought to an end at five thirty on a Saturday morning. Two and a half hours later, the jury returned with the verdict that

Residents of Kingston were undoubtedly stunned to learn that a local man had burned a child to death. *Vintage postcard courtesy of KarenLu LaPolice.*

Brown was guilty of second-degree murder. He was sentenced to six years' imprisonment and a fine of $2,000. In his own defense, Brown had testified that that fire must have been hotter than he thought it was.

During his imprisonment, his first child was born. The next child arrived three years after his release. Sarah went on to have ten more children with Brown, including two sets of twins. Two sons and a daughter died as children.

DR. PERCY SENIOR KILLS TEENAGE GIRL

Young Woman Dies at Hands of Surgeon with a History of Misconduct

The advertisement of Percy Senior ran in several newspapers, including those read by residents of Westerly: "Dr. Percy A. Senior, specialist in diseases of women, twenty-two years' experience primarily in London, for appointment, write him at his office on Main Street in Westerly." Eighteen-year-old Kate Benvenuto got the message.

It was 1914, and Kate lived on Pierce Street with her Italian father, Giovanni "John" Benvenuto; her stepmother, Santa; older brother, Angelo; younger sisters, Theresa, Julia and Susie; and little brother, Charles. Giovanni worked

MURDER

Westerly was home to many physicians; however, few of them violated the law as often as Dr. Percy Senior. *Vintage postcard from the collection of the author.*

in the town's granite quarries and was undoubtedly unaware that the teenage Kate had discovered she was pregnant. She began visiting the office of Dr. Senior quite frequently, and the doctor visited her home very often as well. Area police began noticing this and were suspicious of the behavior. However, it was not until a few months later that they could do anything about it. Word got around town on Wednesday, July 2, that Kate Benvenuto had died that night.

Authorities immediately began investigating the death and determined that Kate had died as the result of an operation. In the cellar of her family's home, police discovered the body of a premature infant. Dr. Senior was promptly arrested. Later, during a hearing at the Third District Court of Westerly, he chose to have no legal representation. Town solicitor Harry B. Agard spoke for the prosecution as it attempted to gain a judge's ruling of probable guilt for abortion and murder. A sentence for murder would have Dr. Senior imprisoned for life. A sentence for abortion, with which no person in Rhode Island had ever been charged before, would find him imprisoned for five to twenty years. After being arraigned, he pleaded not guilty to both charges.

Kate's sister Theresa and brother Angelo were among those who testified for the prosecution, as were Westerly medical examiner Dr. Michael Scanlon and Hopkinton medical examiner Dr. Asa Briggs. Briggs had conducted the autopsy along with Dr. Russell B. Smith and Dr. John L. May.

When the judge asked Dr. Senior if he had any evidence to present or any reason why he should not be found under probable guilt, he asked, "Is the charge murder?"

111

"Yes," replied the judge, "the same upon which you were arraigned and pleaded not guilty."

"Is that the charge now?" the doctor asked.

When informed that it was, he replied, "In that case, the district court cannot accept bail, am I right?"

When he was answered in the affirmative again, he walked to the witness stand and simply stood there in silence with his head bowed for two full minutes. The judge finally spoke up, announcing that he did not wish to disturb Senior's thoughts, but if he had anything to say on his own behalf, he should say it.

"I do not know of anything in particular," Dr. Senior replied, "unless the council for the state wants to question me."

He was informed that the state had no questions, and the judge asked him again if he had anything he wanted to say on his behalf. "No evidence has been introduced to warrant the charge of murder," he stated.

According to the evidence in the case, it ought to be dismissed right now. I might talk for an hour or two, but the result would be the same, for I know the personal feeling of the court against me. No case has been proven of murder, as the prosecution must prove malice, and none has been shown in this case. There is no convicting evidence on that charge. I can prove that the girl was given the best of medical and surgical skill, and I do not consider that I am in any way responsible for her death. I was arrested at half-past six o'clock in the morning while on my way to a market and, in an undressed and unpresentable condition, taken to a cell in the police station. No such action as this could be taken against any other doctor, but I am not a member of the Westerly doctors' trust.

Dr. Senior was judged to be probably guilty and ordered to be held for trial. He was then led out of the room, which held a large attendance of spectators, including his wife and children and Kate's father and stepmother. If the court had a "personal feeling" about him, as he'd suggested, it wasn't without good cause. Dr. Senior was born in England in 1865. A graduate of Cambridge University, he served as a surgeon in Africa during the Boer War before coming to the United States. Living with his second wife, Frances, and their children—twelve-year-old Pearl and six-year-old Winifred—he conducted his services out of an office on Main Street in Westerly, as well as providing services several days per week in other towns such as Newport. He had already been arrested three times that year for being a common drunkard and convicted twice, being found guilty of inebriation and committing indecent acts in public places. Each time, he had been placed on probation. This time, however, he had his license to practice medicine in Rhode Island revoked.

In January 1915, Dr. Senior went up against the State Board of Health to have his license reinstated. Authorities had discovered that, after several people had approached Senior and asked him to perform illegal acts of a medical nature, he had quoted them a price. Due to that, and his history of being charged with gross professional misconduct, his appeal was denied. In April of the following year, he was placed before the United States commissioner in Connecticut on charges that he had violated federal narcotic laws by writing out prescriptions without being registered with the Internal Revenue Service. Dr. Senior admitted that he had been visiting an old patient and had a right to treat him under Connecticut statutes. Feigning ignorance, he argued that he had never been formally told that, after his license to practice medicine in Rhode Island was revoked, it was also revoked by federal authorities. After the hearing, Dr. Senior was hauled off to jail.

ELIZA SMITH AND HER CHILDREN ARE FOUND DEAD IN A WELL

A Disappearance Leads to a Gruesome Discovery

North Kingstown farmer Jeremiah Smith opened his eyes on the morning of July 8, 1870. It was very early, and his five-year-old son, William, with whom he shared a bed, was still asleep. Jeremiah quietly made his way out of the room and into the kitchen, where, strangely, the back door was unlocked. In the window that faced the backyard, a light had been lit and cast a glow outside. Jeremiah opened the door. "Eliza?" he called. There was no answer. Stepping out into the morning air, he looked around the immediate area, thinking perhaps his wife had gone outside for some reason. He did not find Eliza, but when he glanced toward the rainwater cistern about twenty feet away from the door, he noticed that the cover was off of it. He had gotten water the night before and figured he must have forgotten to replace the cover, as he had done many times before. He picked up the cover from the ground and replaced it over the cistern before going back into the house.

Those living in Slocum and the other villages of North Kingstown were aghast to learn the nightmarish fate of Eliza Smith and her children. *Vintage postcard courtesy of KarenLu LaPolice.*

Jeremiah went into the bedroom where his three-year-old daughter, Mary Eliza, and his two-and-a-half-month-old baby boy, Jeremiah, slept. The bedding was rumpled where the children had lain, but they were not there. Jeremiah became concerned and realized that something was terribly wrong. He walked to the house of his neighbor, Mr. Franklin, and asked him if he had seen Eliza and the children. When Franklin replied that he had not, Jeremiah told him they were gone and asked Franklin if he would help search for them.

Immediately, the two men left Franklin's house. Franklin went straight to Jeremiah's house, while Jeremiah headed in the direction of his father-in-law's place. He hoped Eliza's parents, George Washington Northup and Mary Taylor (Gardiner), might know where his wife and children were. They didn't, and George returned to Jeremiah's house with him. As they approached the yard, they could see Franklin still searching the premises. When they got within hearing distance, George told him, "Look in the cistern. I believe she is in there."

The cistern sat atop a curb that was two feet higher than the ground. Constructed of aged wooden boards, it had a square opening at the top

114

that measured eighteen inches and then tapered down to thirteen inches. The bottom part of the opening hung about three feet from the top of the water, which measured about four feet deep. The early morning hour and the darkness inside the cistern made it difficult for Franklin to see inside. However, he saw what he believed to be the material of an infant's dress floating on the water. The men went and secured some hooks, which they attached to the dress. As they pulled the hooks up, the dead body of little Jeremiah was revealed. They continued to fish around in the cistern until the bodies of Mary and Eliza had been pulled out as well.

Authorities searched for answers. Jeremiah reported that nothing out of the ordinary had taken place the previous evening. Eliza had gotten the children ready for bed and hung their day clothes in the usual place. The only thing that had struck him as odd was when, the day before, he had noticed three ropes secreted away in the yard. One of the ropes was a clothesline, and the other two had been removed from the well, where they had been utilized in pulling up chilled butter. He now wondered if his wife had hidden the three ropes with the intention of hanging herself and the two children.

Eliza was known for having a nervous disposition and being totally incapable of handling the slightest bit of discourse in life. Neighbors told

The railroad station in Slocum, a village of North Kingstown. *Vintage postcard courtesy of KarenLu LaPolice.*

authorities that there had been difficulties in the marriage, and the fact that the couple slept in separate bedrooms made police wonder whether their marital state had anything to do with the tragedy. They finally decided it did not and that Eliza had simply gone temporarily insane. They theorized that she had waited until her husband had fallen asleep and then probably made two trips out to the cistern, carrying the children from their bedroom, through the sitting room and the kitchen. Still, no one could figure out how a thirty-three-year-old woman had forced herself through a thirteen-inch opening. A trough that extended into the opening more than half an inch hadn't even been disturbed, and none of the rotting boards that held the cistern together had been wrenched apart in any way. Eliza's arms were bruised and scraped near her elbows, most likely due to the friction of passing through the cistern opening, but there were no other marks on her body. Having never readied herself for bed, she was still wearing her dress, which was pinned up at the sleeves, as they were whenever she did housework. However, she was not wearing shoes or stockings.

Eliza, Mary and Jeremiah were buried in Elm Grove Cemetery in North Kingstown. The cistern, about a mile from Slocumville, would be a tragic reminder of that terrible summer morning in 1870—one that five-year-old William would have to live with for the rest of his life as he and his father carried on.

A&P MANAGER WITNESSES BODY OF HARRY BREWER FALLING INTO GUTTER

A Murder Victim Is Dragged Behind a Car for Miles

Harry Lester Brewer of Mystic, Connecticut, had a court hearing coming up on March 29, 1943, due to a recent suicide attempt. The forty-year-old employee of Roniteau Mills in Ashaway and his wife, Clara (Pierce), had endured the accidental death of their son Harry just a little over a month earlier. The eleven-year-old had drowned in Shunuc Brook in North Stonington, and Harry became so despondent that his drinking habit spiraled out of control. One morning, toward the middle of March, he tried to kill himself and landed in the Westerly Hospital. He remained in the hospital the rest of that day and part of the next before he was released to go home. He returned to work the following day, a Wednesday, and fulfilled his employment hours on Thursday and Friday as well. Although he was scheduled to work on Saturday, too, he told his wife that he had somewhere to go and that he would not return until noontime on Monday. However, that evening, his dead body was discovered lying in a Westerly gutter.

James Panciera, an undertaker who resided on Friendship Street in Westerly, and his friend Donald Raffo of Garden Street in Pawcatuck were driving across the bridge from Stonington in Panciera's car when the headlights shone on something lying in the gutter on Canal Street. The men got out of the car to investigate. The body was warm, and Panciera checked for signs of life. In just a few moments, they were joined by Salvatore Sanquedolce of Pleasant Street in Westerly. Sanquedolce had been working at the A&P on the corner of Pleasant Street and Canal Street, where he was employed as manager, when he saw a car, which was dragging something, pass by the store. He told Panciera and Raffo that the object was attached to the bumper, and he saw it fall off. "It looked like a pig," he stated and was shocked to now see that it was a human being. When police arrived, Sanquedolce told them the car was a large sedan, and it had been heading in the direction of White Rock.

The body was examined by authorities, who found the skull crushed and the flesh raw with road burns. The jaw, thighs, legs and numerous other bones were broken. One arm bared a tattoo spelling out "Harry L. Brewer,

The body of Harry Brewer fell from a vehicle that was headed toward White Rock, the village where the White Rock Mill stood. *Vintage postcard courtesy of KarenLu LaPolice.*

Staffordville, December 17, 1902." When the socks and shoes were removed from the body, it was discovered that there was sand on and inside the shoes. One of the few sandy roads in the area was Chase Hill Road in Hopkinton, and the following day, clothes were found strung along that very road, torn to shreds. The road was roped off, the police visited area bars to question the locals and all of Brewer's relatives were rounded up for questioning. It was learned that the last place any of the witnesses had seen Brewer was in Ashaway at ten o'clock on Saturday morning. According to friends and family members, he was a good worker with a good personality but had a habit of becoming disagreeable when he was drinking. The autopsy showed that his stomach contained no food and a very small amount of alcohol, which was believed to be cider.

Authorities theorized that perhaps someone had accidentally hit Brewer with their car and then dragged him down the road. The body had been pulled over dirt, as well as pavement, as could be determined by his shoes. His wallet, which was found along with his clothing, had a hole worn through one side from the friction of being dragged. One of Brewer's teeth was also discovered along the same stretch of road. It was finally thought to be more likely that his death had been the result of murder as opposed to an accident. Police surmised that Brewer had been killed somewhere near Chase Hill Road and then taken in the direction of the Pawcatuck River, where the killer was going to dispose of him. They believed that, at some point, the body had been put in the trunk but partially fell out and was dragged along the road before dropping off into the gutter. However, there were no witnesses, no suspects and no motive.

The son of Lester and Ida Brewer, the victim had grown up in Mystic, Connecticut, where his father worked as a woolen mill carder. His parents divorced, and he and his five siblings were raised by his father. He had previously worked as a laborer for the railroad and spent many years employed by the Swift River Woolen Company in Potter Hill. Up until March 3, he had been employed at Electric Boat. For reasons no one knew, he quit that job and soon gained employment at Roniteau Mills. He had no enemies that anyone knew of—certainly no one who would do something as brutal as kill him and drag his dead body down the road for miles behind a car. There didn't seem to be any logical answers concerning why this man, in deep mourning for the child he had lost, would find his own life ended in such a nightmarish manner.

MURDER

EZRA HOLLOWAY IS KILLED BY PIRATES
North Kingstown Grave Puzzles Many

There is a gravestone in North Kingstown's Elm Grove Cemetery that has ignited the interest of passersby for decades. The stone tells us that Eldred Holloway "fell victim to the assassin on board of the Brigantine *Crawford* near the island of Cuba, June 1, 1827." Holloway was, in fact, killed by a cohort of one of the most famous pirates in history. During the early nineteenth century, due to the presence of American and British ships in the waters around Spain, pirates eventually discovered that it was easier to take over a ship if they were able to actually sail on it, gaining the trust of all aboard before staging their attack. Acting as mere passengers or seamen, the pirates were able to put themselves in the perfect position for a successful mutiny.

The *Crawford* was an American ship under the command of an asthmatic captain, Henry Brightman of Troy, Massachusetts, who often struggled to breathe and had to subdue attacks of coughing. The ship had been loaded up with rum, sugar, coffee and molasses on the Cuban seaport island of Matanzas and set sail for New York on May 28, 1827. Fifteen passengers were aboard, including three Spanish men and a Frenchman who boarded at Matanzas and claimed to be sailors. On the morning of May 31, the Frenchman approached the ship's African American cook, Stephen Gibbs, and began instructing him on the proper way to fry eggs. The cook became annoyed with the intrusion. He explained that he knew how to fry eggs and asked the man to go away. The Frenchman would not relent. He finally slipped his hand into the pocket of his coat and then withdrew it, a yellowish powder secured between his thumb and forefinger. Sprinkling it over the eggs, he explained that this "native pepper" should always be used in frying eggs. Angered, the cook picked up a spoon and attempted to scrape the powder away. Little did the cook know that this man was the infamous pirate Alexander Tardy, who had long kept authorities on the chase. The fifty-seven-year-old Tardy usually boarded ships claiming to be a doctor. He had actually practiced dentistry in Havana before moving on to a life of crime on the high seas. He spoke several languages and preferred to poison his victims.

Not long after breakfast, everyone on board except for Tardy and the Spaniards was overcome with drowsiness. By nightfall, they were vomiting profusely. Exhaustion took over, and they eventually decided to lay out their bedding and retire for the evening. At two o'clock the following morning, first mate Edward Dobson was awakened by the sound of screams. Thinking the ship had collided with something, he rushed up on deck, where he saw

Rhode Island has close ties with pirate tales, and Eldred Holloway, whose gravestone stands in North Kingstown, lost his life at the hands of swashbucklers. *Image of* The Buccaneers, *painted by Frederick Judd Waugh circa 1906, courtesy of the Library of Congress.*

seamen Joseph Doliver of Salem, Massachusetts, and Oliver Potter of Westport, Massachusetts, run past him, screaming as if in immense pain. Suddenly, one of the Spaniards appeared and thrust a knife into his shoulder. Dobson ran from his attacker toward the direction of the cabin, but as he approached, Brightman stepped through the cabin door, reeled around from the effects of a recent stab wound to the neck and then fell to the floor with a thud. His body was promptly thrown overboard.

Dobson quickly followed in the footsteps of Doliver and Potter, who were spotting the deck with their blood. As they ran around the ship, Potter grew weaker. A gaping stab wound in his abdomen would no longer allow his intestines to remain contained, and the other men were aware that he would soon be dead. After climbing high up a masthead, the men watched the Spaniards, armed with muskets, walk over to the forecastle and summon Bicknell, who was below decks. Bicknell, moaning loudly, obeyed their command. He had already been stabbed as well and secured a makeshift bandage around his abdomen. The moment he stepped up onto the deck, the pirates aimed their muskets and fired. Bicknell fell dead. Dobson's attention to the shooting was pulled away by screams coming from the water below. He ran to the side of the ship and looked out into the darkness, where two men had chosen to jump overboard—a passenger named Nathan and the owner of the cargo, Norman Robinson. Treading water, they yelled, "Please, please, throw us a barrel, a plank, an oar, anything to save our lives!" The pirates gave no response, and soon, Dobson watched both men slip beneath the surface of the water. Tardy turned and gazed up at Dobson and Doliver. He told them to climb back down, and their lives would be spared. The men complied. Immediately, pirates Jose "Pepe" Cesares and Jose "Courro" Morando grabbed Doliver, cut his throat and flung him overboard. Potter expired while trying to keep his grip on the masthead and dropped lifelessly into the sea. Gibbs, who had also climbed to safety, was ordered to come down.

Eldred Holloway, an Irish carpenter from Providence, had already been killed and thrown overboard. Connecticut seaman Asa Bicknell had been shot and cast into the sea along with two passengers, leaving just Dobson, Gibbs and a Frenchman named Ferdinand Ginoulhiac alive. Tardy needed able men to navigate the ship. Provisions on board were getting low, and it had become necessary to dock somewhere to obtain food and water. The pirates obliterated the ship's name from the stern and destroyed its authentic papers. Cuban authorities had provided them with falsified papers, which stated that the ship was Spanish property. This would allow them to sail on to Hamburg, where they could sell both the vessel and its cargo.

At about six o'clock on the night of June 5, they dropped anchor at Old Point Comfort on the Capes of Virginia. Dobson was ordered to lower a boat and go ashore to obtain supplies. Such a risk proved poor planning on Tardy's part. Dobson ran to Fortress Monroe and quickly told the officers there of the mutiny. They followed him back to shore and across the water toward the ship. Realizing his plan had failed, Tardy picked up a knife and slit his own throat. Cesares, Morando and Felix Barbeito had already removed a small boat from a nearby vessel and set sail. Word spread about the pirate attack, and a massive search was begun for the trio. The customhouse officer took custody of the brigantine and sent it to Norfolk. The pirates were soon captured in the Isle of Wight County and put in the Hampton jail. As the three surviving passengers gave details of the mutiny, the Spaniards declared it was all untrue. They blamed Tardy solely and swore to their own innocence. On August 17, cloaked in purple hooded robes, all three sat on empty coffins as they rode in a wagon to the hanging place. When the trapdoors were sprung, the ropes of Cesares and Morando snapped, and they had to be re-hanged. The bodies were later buried but eventually unearthed for experimental use.

Eldred Holloway had been in Matanzas on business for several months. Cesares had bragged to one of the surviving passengers that he had had the honor of killing Holloway with his own hands. Undoubtedly, the braggart was the assassin forever noted on Holloway's grave.

POLICE OFFICER JOSEPH WESTLAKE IS GUNNED DOWN BY SOLDIER

A Fatal Shot at Narragansett Pier Ends a Lawman's Life

Narragansett Pier had always been a busy place during the summer months, and that Friday evening of August 22, 1902, was no different. Thirty-one-year-old army private William Lacey and two fellow soldiers stationed at Fort Greble were visiting the pier that night. Members of the Seventy-second Company of Artillery, they had decided to head back toward their barracks at about half-past midnight, and as they left the pier, they were allegedly accosted by two men named McCrea and McNulty outside of a bar. Several gunshots suddenly rang out as the tramps were fired at, attracting the attention of two pier police officers on duty that evening. Officer John Wright and Officer Joseph Westlake had been walking their beat along the pier near the casino when the shots rang out. They ran in the direction of the assault and chased after Westlake when he and another soldier, Edward Clements, tried to flee. Suddenly, without warning, Private Lacey fired two shots at the officers. One bullet struck Wright in the forehead, causing a serious head wound. The other entered the left side of Westlake's abdomen, lodging in his back near the spine. Wright rushed at Lacey, striking him with a billy club and breaking his jaw and nose. Lacey and the other soldier were arrested and jailed in Kingston while doctors called to the scene dressed Westlake's wound and had him transported to the hospital. His chances of recovery were considered to be slight, and he died soon after.

Thirty-two-year-old Westlake was a native of England. He had been married for eight years, and he and his wife, Ellen, had a seven-year-old son named Walter and a baby boy named George at home on Point Judith Road. The following month, Lacey stood trail for Westlake's murder at the Washington County Courthouse in Kingston. He claimed that the fatal

The casino at Narragansett Pier, where police officer Joseph Westlake was killed by a soldier. *Photograph taken circa 1899, courtesy of the Library of Congress.*

shooting had been an accident, and after the jurors had been selected and sworn in, they were taken to the scene of the crime. Clements, who was serving an eighteen-month sentence for desertion in a military prison in Kentucky, was brought back to Rhode Island as a government witness in the trial. Before long, Lacey was locked up at the military prison within Fort Adams in Newport, where he would spend a good many years for his crime.

MURDER OF TINDARO PINTO AT THE SCHOOL FOR THE FEEBLE-MINDED
Little Boy Is Found Stuffed into Laundry Bag

The Joseph Ladd School in Exeter, once known as the Rhode Island School for the Feeble-Minded, became a house of horrors during the twentieth century when overcrowding took its toll. The 475-acre Hoxsie Farm had been purchased by the state in 1907 for the purpose of starting the school. At its beginning, it housed eight mentally retarded boys. Before long, over five thousand inmates were crammed into every available nook and cranny. Over the years, there were charges of experimentation, neglect and an insufficient number of staff members. Then, in 1955, there was a charge of murder.

Many experts on the subject of mental disability didn't see much point in helping the afflicted to progress or to enjoy a good quality of life. It was believed that they simply needed to be separated from society for the reason of protecting the public and keeping the mentally disabled from reproducing and perhaps adding more undesirable traits to the gene pool. Such children, many felt, did nothing but place a burden on their parents and society alike. They were referred to as "poor unfortunates," "imbeciles," "backward children" and "idiots." The nightmare that many of these children and adults lived through can only be imagined.

On October 18, 1955, police were called to the Ladd School when staff members alerted them to a situation at the Howe House, the building where inmates with mild mental afflictions were housed. There, on the floor of the shower room, lay a laundry bag with a body inside. According to records, a nine-year-old inmate named Tindaro Pinto had been acting unruly that

The School for the Feeble-Minded in Exeter, also known as Ladd School, where young Tindaro Pinto was suffocated in a laundry bag. *Vintage postcard courtesy of KarenLu LaPolice.*

day and annoying a fifty-one-year-old female dining room attendant known only as Mrs. D. The attendant had been employed at the school for about sixteen years, and Pinto had been residing there for nearly five. His behavior, she felt, was cause for punishment. She pulled aside a twenty-year-old male inmate—a lifelong ward of the state and a court-committed delinquent. She ordered him to shove Pinto into a laundry bag and hang the bag from one of the shower nozzles. The inmate did as he was told, and those in the vicinity of the shower room could hear the little boy screaming for about two hours. Then the screams stopped. Staff members who later went into the shower room at about 4:30 p.m. took the bag down and yanked the top open, as the weight of Pinto's body had pulled the drawstrings so tight that virtually no air was being allowed into the bag. The child, who had turned blue, drew in two loud gasps of air and then died. Mrs. D. was charged with murder but made a deal that allowed her to serve just three years in the state prison.

The horrific deaths at Ladd School did not stop with the brutal killing of Pinto. Gerard Picard, a South Kingstown native, had been admitted to the school at the age of twenty-two in 1968. Diagnosed with Down's syndrome and mental retardation, he was visited regularly by his family until one day in 1971 when his uncle was turned away by a staff member, who told him that Picard was ill and not receiving visitors. The man returned the following week and demanded to see his nephew. What he observed was troubling. Picard appeared very ill and very afraid. When Picard's sister learned of this, she visited the school with a friend who was a nurse. The nurse determined that Picard was running a fever and had very peculiar burns marks on his buttocks that had been left untreated. When they inquired about what was being done to help Picard through his bout of illness, a staff member informed them that he was simply being given aspirin. Picard's sister demanded that he be given the proper medical care he needed. When Picard died on June 27 of that year, the death certificate sent to the family stated that he had died at the state hospital due to congestive heart failure and respiratory arrest. Yet medical records told a different story, stating that death had been caused by an untreated staph infection that continued to spread until it weakened his entire body.

It was learned that one Friday, during the early part of that summer, Picard had been taken from the Howe House to the school's Fogarty Building clinic with pelvic and leg pains. The weekend relief doctor on duty that day determined that Picard had a blood infection and began treatments. He also noted the burns on Picard's buttocks, which he described as looking as if he had been forced to sit on a hot barbecue grill. The regular medical staff did not continue with the treatments, and a serious blood infection ensued. When later questioned about why the treatments were stopped, one of the doctors explained that "extraordinary measures" were not taken to save the mentally retarded.

On June 30, 1972, a twenty-eight-year-old inmate of Ladd School named Robert Dill died of an undiagnosed skull fracture. Dill had been lying comatose for six days, and no medical attention had been afforded him. Henry Okun, a sixty-year-old inmate, had been complaining to the staff of throat pain for a long period of time before he was transferred to Rhode Island Hospital. He died there on October 16, 1976, of cancer of the larynx, a condition that could have been successfully treated much earlier. However, the refusal to provide Okun with any medical care at the school had allowed the condition to reach a fatal stage. By that time, the tumor had reached the size of an apple and had ruptured.

A teenage inmate named Douglas Dodd suffered with severe pain for eighteen months. Blocked-up excrement in his body had left his abdomen bloated and rock hard; however, he received no medical attention at all until just hours before his death on June 17, 1979. Another man, an unidentified inmate in his mid-fifties, lay bleeding to death at the school for almost four weeks before he died. Doctors refused to give him the transfusions to save his life, later explaining that it had been a "mercy killing."

Charges of medical neglect racked up at the school for years and were determined to be the cause of nearly a dozen inmate deaths.

SOURCES

Ancestry.com
Assorted Rhode Island City directories
Chariho (RI) Times
The Day (CT)
Evening Telegraph (PA)
Familysearch.org
Findagrave.com
Genealogy.com
Hope Valley (RI) Advertiser
The Hour (CT)
Library of Congress
Narragansett Police Department
Narragansett (RI) Times
New England Paranormal Research
Norwich (CT) Bulletin
Officer Down Memorial Page
Providence (RI) News
Representative Men & Old Families of Rhode Island. Providence, RI: J.H. Beers & Company, 1908.
Rhode Island Historical Cemeteries Transcription Project
Rhode Island State Archives
RI Genweb
Rootsweb.com
State of Rhode Island and Providence Plantations Superior Court records
Wikimedia Commons
Wikipedia.org

ABOUT THE AUTHOR

Kelly Sullivan Pezza is a native of Hope Valley, Rhode Island, and has worked as a journalist for Southern Rhode Island Newspapers for seventeen years. With an education in law enforcement and many years of experience as a Rhode Island historian and genealogist, she has written hundreds of articles and several books concerning historic true crime and unsolved mysteries in Rhode Island.

In addition to her works of nonfiction, such as *History, Mystery & Lore of Rhode Island*; *Murder at Rocky Point Park*; and *Hidden History of South County, Rhode Island*, Pezza has also published two fictional dramatic novels: *Snowglobe* and *The Rarest Beautiful*.

The winner of the Kraft National Writing Award and the New England Press Award, she provided a portion of the historical narration for the acclaimed documentary *You Must Be This Tall: The Story of Rocky Point*, produced by documentary filmmaker David Bettencourt in 2007, and will also provide some narration for film producer Jason Mayoh's Rocky Point documentary, due out in 2015.

Currently, she is lecturing on local history at area organizations, libraries and schools while working on her next novel.

CPSIA information can be obtained
at www.ICGtesting.com
Printed in the USA
LVHW041312010920
664725LV00017B/1416